PIMP-N THE PEN

WHILE DOING THE ONE THING
BY:
RICHARD SPRAGGINS

Richard Spraggins

Copyright © 2020 Richard Spraggins

All rights reserved.

First print 2020 June

No portion of this book may be reproduced in any form, or by any means without prior permission from the author and publisher, as a collective, except for quotes used in reviews or as permitted by U.S. copyright law.

ISBN: 978-0-578-65994-7

To purchase email: FreeToCreate2020@gmail.com

For permissions contact:
Free To Create
PO BOX 494375
Garland, TX 75049-4375
972-698-4702

FreeToCreate2020@gmail.com

Book Cover: Free To Create

Book Production: Free To Create

ACKNOWLEDGMENTS

I would like to endorse my highest respect (to the superlative degree) to all the convicts who are currently behind the wall that refuses to press the STOP button on their lives. In a world filled to the capacity with mediocrity and paralyzed men who clearly have broken spines along with Kool-Aid pumpin through their veins. You, on the other hand, not only have the courage, but the bold audacity to do something different besides the common, run-of-the-mill bullshit crim1nals been chasing basically since the dawn of time. You took off like a rocket while mostly everyone else around you are jogging to monotonous speeds on treadmills...

GOING NOWHERE AT ALL!

Kenneth (Kenny The Barber) Garner, you are the epitome of the three words: NEVER GIVE UP! And I raise my right hand to my head with a two-finger salute to your non-stop grind and pure conviction that you put down, not allowing PRISON to determine or dictate your true destiny in life. You didn't fold, nor did you conform to the norm by trapping yourself to a domino or knock table, sports TV, or chasing the game. You didn't come in here (prison) with the conventional pipe-dream fantasy of deeming it necessary to win a CO or chase K-2 products like a dope fiend with his head cut off. Nah, you saw it more important to remain a factor in your boy's (children) lives, stay positive, and adamant about putting something down that will benefit you in the long run. You wrote book after book and worked on project after project (and even wrote a Children's Book about your boys). NOW THAT'S GANGSTA!

So I would like to ask the average convict who is currently reading this acknowledgment: Does this sound a little far-fetched? A little hard to imagine just yet. So was the creative vision of so many other convicts on the Allred Unit when my dude first put it down. The prison world didn't yet realize that writing books (and actually getting published) was ripe for reimagining. But when Kenny The Barber DID IT, he set the bar for the whole unit to follow.

My challenge now, however, is no more and no less, so I'm calling my shot here, today, as I did then:

    I GOT NEXT!

Positive – over – Negative

Greatness -over- Mediocrity

Driven -over- Lazy

Winning -over- Losing

Contents

Chapter		Page
1.	The Five P's	7
2.	State of Mind	12
	TITLES	18
3.	The Game is Over	19
	CRIME VS. LEGIT RECIDIVISM STATISTICS	28
4.	Master Your Environment	30
	ARE YOU 14 YEARS OLD?	47
5.	Bread and Circuses	49
	SLAVES TO THE DEVIL'S	56
6.	Color Blind	57
7.	Stuck in a Time Warp	60
	WILLIE LYNCH SYNDROME	63
	MESSAGE TO THE REAL NIGGA	69
	BRAIN TEASER: THE LIGHT SWITCH	71
8.	The One Thing	73
	MALCOLM X	78
	WAHIDA CLARK	86
	MIKE ENEMIGO	91
	COSS MARTE	99

DONALD RAY JOHNSON, SHANNON HOLMES, JEFF HENDERSON, DARIUS CLARK MONROE, SEAN PICA, JAYDA RASBERRY, and MARLON PETERSON — 101-104

RICARD SPRAGGINS' INTERVIEW — 105-109

INTRODUCTION

FOR WHOM THIS BOOK WAS WRITTEN

Pimp-N The Pen was written exclusively for you: the convict who is currently residing behind these prison walls, navigating time while maneuvering around bullshit. However, one of the unfortunate challenges facing convicts regarding doing time is this nonchalant myth that our culture keeps perpetuating. Some Vicks in here look at doing time and shrug their shoulders, "So what if I got a bid, I'll bounce back as soon as I touch down," as if there is not a huge gap missing out of our lives and "Bouncing Back" is just a mere snap of the fingers. Though I realize that some people can't see past their hands. The street mentality needs that instant gratification, and that's why most of us became criminals in the first place because we couldn't see past the "right now." If we would have developed just maybe a small glimpse of a vision towards the future, then, believe me, we certainly would not be part of the fastest-growing, most recession-proof industry in America. Being as how the prison industry is a sure bet for those who profit from it.

I've come to understand (for the most part) that there is a very low awareness level amongst convicts. Many of us have fallen for myths that have been given to us by a mass media BEAST that profits from our weak choices. This Beast teaches capitalism, not achievement. Yet we allow the media to continuously sell us a lifestyle that does not include education, raising our seed, good health, morals, and greatness. Still, most people in here have this "You can pull yourself up by your bootstraps" myth about prison.
Likewise, there is a real gap between this myth and the reality for those who are actually trying to overcome criminal addiction in the process of juggling all this time on our hands. So my main purpose for writing this book is so I could pull the curtain back—therefore, raising your level of consciousness so you can see, plus develop a bird's eye view on all your actions while you are doing this bid.

One of the necessary questions I want to ask you is:

WHAT ARE YOU TAKING ADVANTAGE OF?

Before you answer that question, let me lace you up and paraphrase from the English Dictionary of what TAKING ADVANTAGE OF actually means. According to Webster's New World Dictionary, TO TAKE ADVANTAGE OF is defined as:

1) to use for one's own benefit.

2) to profit from.

Now, I don't have the slightest clue of what your charge is, but I I know that you have a pretty good idea of what it means to use someone (or something) for your own personal benefit. Likewise, I don't have a degree from Harvard University, but I know that I am highly qualified to drop a few jewels on these relevant issues based on my life experience alone. So, writing this book is also my catalytic way of giving back to society (considering everything I took away from it) because guess what? Both of us are going to eventually return back to society.

Anyway, I have a disarming habit of interrupting my own conversations and saying, "That's a point I want to come back to later," like a congressman making sure a statement enters into the official record. But in the meantime, what I want you to understand and fully get a gist of is the fact that we all manipulate each other to get what we want to some degree, even as children.

It's a natural human instinct. The way I see it, the only difference between a con-man and a stockbroker on Wall Street is that one cons people out of hundreds of dollars and the other cons people out of millions of dollars. Basically, the oldest Pimp Game on earth is the same as what builds nations: the control of money and people to achieve an objective. Only thing is, these days, you have to be smart, move with finesse, plan your moves strategically, and never lose focus of the one thing.

No matter how old you are or how many years you've been down, this book should be considered as HEAT to place in your arsenal of weaponry to battle against mediocrity. Because as things go, age and wisdom do not have a direct correlation. You, on the other hand, are inevitably linked to PRISON and TIME. That's why I have to abruptly switch gears right quick because I just remembered the point I need to get back to:

HOW ARE YOU TAKING ADVANTAGE OF YOUR PRISON TIME?
THAT WHICH WILL BENEFIT YOU WHEN YOU TOUCHDOWN?

If the doors opened up to you right now today, what could you say that you have (or have done) to show for doing X number of years in a prison system that couldn't care less if you stared at the walls twirling your thumbs the whole time you were here? If by chance, you can't answer this question, then the new insight in reading this book will guide you on your journey to the goals you will see fit to accomplish, the vision you will desire to have, and the overall BOSS that you will most definitely realize that you are. Moreover, you will be equipped with the fundamental tools and the essential mind state it's going to take to

PIMP THE PEN IN THE SAME MATTER THAT IT
PIMPED YOU!

Chapter 1

THE FIVE Ps

If you're like most convicts, you've spent a lot of your time on the inside fantasizing about what your life will be like when you finally touch down. Maybe the first thing you plan to do is eat a juicy, filet mignon steak with all the sides, or make passionate love to your girl, possibly hug your kids, or even enjoy the stars through the panoramic moon roof of your brand new whip.

Beyond those first days of freedom, you've probably even imagined getting swagged up in a fresh new unit, stimulated by a fresh new start. Having served your bid, you hope that people (including your family and friends) will give you a chance to prove that you're a changed man, headed in a new direction. This time you're going to get it right: find a new job, work hard, and take care of your family, ... right?

Unfortunately, without proper preparation for life on the outside, even the most optimistic and determined of ex-convicts can stumble, come up short, fall flat on their faces and end up back in the yard. And as for that great job you were thinking about, working at McDonald's wasn't really what you had in mind, now was it? Your weekly paycheck is hardly enough to cover your grocery bill, let alone your rent, while your girl has an expensive shopping habit. Faced with this grim economic reality, you find yourself tempted to get back to the grind, where money was good, easy, fast, and you damn sure never had to ask, "Do you want fries with that?"

Unless you were unfortunately sentenced to death or Life Without, then sooner or later you are going to get out of prison. It's common for all of us behind the wall to fantasize about what we're going to do when we finally get out. We dream about sex, driving choice cars, wearing first-rate designer clothes (both inspired by what we saw while flipping through a GQ and a Robb Report magazine). Oh yeah, and don't forget about owning that million-dollar business. One thousand apologies for being the one to tell you, but it's time for a reality check. You need to fully understand that by simply becoming a felon, the cards are stacked highly against you. In today's world, it is perfectly legal to discriminate against criminals in nearly every way in the United States of America. Once you are labeled with a felony jacket, the old forms of discrimination become prevalent: employment discrimination, housing discrimination, denial of food stamps, public benefits, and exclusion from jury service. You WILL NOT be able to vote and don't even think about owning a firearm.

This is why it's important to construct a post-release plan that anticipates the problem you are going to face. Procrastinating and waiting gets you nowhere really quick. Most of us go through life as failures because we are waiting for the time to be right. "I'll wait until I get out to do all that." So how much time are you going to waste looking back and thinking of what you coulda - woulda - shoulda - done while you were here doing this bid? The best time is always NOW. Therefore, start now where you stand and work with what you have to prepare yourself for your second return because if you don't know, I'll be the one to tell you, PROPER PREPARATION PREVENTS POOR PERFORMANCE.

Tell you what you can do. Survey 50 people that live on your wing and ask them what they want the most when they're released from prison, and I bet you at least 48 of them will not be able to tell you.

Don't get me wrong, you will hear the usual answer. Some will say to be rich, a few will say to own their own business, others will say fame and power, a rap career, to drive a Benz, to own a yacht. Still, others will say ease in living, a wife, take care of their children, to work in the oil field, but none of them (but maybe a few) will be able to define these terms or give the slightest indication of a mapped-out plan by which they hope to come upon these dreamlike wishes. Money, peace, nor happiness respond to wishes. They only respond to clear-cut plans, backed up by clear-cut desires. Thoughts, plans, and desires must be set in motion—POINT BLANK PERIOD!

In other words, your actions right now have to match up with the plans that you have for your release. No matter if you have mere intentions on becoming a plumber, use this precious time to master ALL the aspects of piping and fixtures that a plumber uses for repairs and installations. How that works is:

1) Sign up for a trade that pertains to plumbing.
2) Ask your people to send you information after information about plumbing so that you can at least become enlightened about what you intend to do.

Make better use of your resources (family support) and the internet with valuable information that will assist you with this endeavor. Rap lyrics, urban novels, and Kill-Shots are all irrelevant towards your intended goal.

If you want the best when you get out, then you have to do your best right now. The convict in here who's doing his best is never a failure. He's always a winner, even if the best was something so small as getting his GED. Still, the world will place the victory belt around his waist and raise his hands in the air when he accomplishes it. The convict in here who's doing his best is never a quitter or a loser either because he stayed tight to the right on his job until the best was all there was to give at that particular time. Individuals like this can never be failures.

The convict in here who's doing his best, you'll never hear him asking the classic convict question, "I'm in prison; what's the use?" He doesn't care a whole lot about where he is, his mind is fixed on the idea that he's ON HIS JOB and won't be satisfied with anything less than his best. Why?

Because that's what BOSSES do—we give our best no matter the circumstances or where we might be.

Circumstances don't make the convict—they only reveal the BOSS within him. But this cursed, "I'm in prison; what's the use?" question seems to have been brought to light by some pessimistic, weak, depressed spirit of darkness to use in discouraging convicts behind bars in making desperate struggles to push the STOP button on their lives. I've seen it bring down a lot of convicts in here into that hopelessness, beyond-repair funk.

Thoughts of "Fuck the world" attitudes seems like it's the only option when "Prepare for the world" somehow got placed on the backburner. Push this way of thinking out of your mind whenever it pops up and replaces it with one solid question:

AM I DOING MY BEST?

So, I ask you, "are you doing your best?" How are you taking advantage of your time? What projects are you working on? When dayroom hours are available, what is the first thing (other than a shower) that you do? Does the TV call your name? If so, what's capturing your attention? Not too long ago, I sat down on the front bench next to a convict by the name of Rough-House. He was watching TV when I asked him, "Rough-House, my dude if you don't mind me asking, but what motivates you to watch sitcoms at 7:00 o'clock in the morning?"

He gave me a cold side glance, and I was hoping like hell he didn't detect any sarcasm in my voice. But he just turned his attention back towards the TV, then said, "Because this is how I stay in-tuned and caught-up with the world." He let out a half chuckle as if he thought what I asked was a dumb ass question. "That's what's up!" is all I said as I walked back to my pen and pad at a nearby table. But when I caught a glimpse at the other available TV in the dayroom, I asked myself,

If Rough-House really wanted to stay tuned in to the world like he said, then why wasn't he sitting in front of the other available TV watching THE WORLD NEWS instead of a 20-something-year-old "FRIENDS" rerun?

At that moment, I learned more about the difference between the quitter and the solid convict in here who's doing his best. No one is dead until his heart stops beating, and no one has failed as long as there is one more bit of fight left in him. As soon as (and I repeat this) as soon as any convict behind bars think it's ok to relax and "CHILL" right in the middle of a fight for his life, he has lost all hope for survival.

There's not a better time than now to realize that you're not a failure in life. Just a minor setback for a major come back. One of the vital facts that you have to get a gist of is that by simply being here in prison, you have an advantage. The essence of all time well spent is that it helps you experience the peace, dignity, and positive potential of your own true nature. Therefore, you have to realize that you have the advantage and the power to change a negative situation into a positive outcome.

It's a proven fact that you can take just about any negative and change it into a positive one. If black people in America can take a racial slur such as "NIGGER" and convert it to a comradery like "MY NIGGA," then it brings truth to the theory that things, situations, and circumstances are only how one sees it. Pac saw the negative word as NEVER IGNORANT GETTING GOALS ACCOMPLISHED. So what I'm trying to figure out is why we can't take a negative environment like a prison and convert it into something positive as well. Prison is only how one sees it. PREVENT RECIDIVISM IS SEEKING OPPORTUNITY NOW. Ask me, and I'll tell you that prison is a great opportunity.

When the opportunity comes, it appears in a different form, and from a different direction than most people might expect. Yeah, that's right, even opportunity has a tendency to manipulate people because that's one of the deceitful gimmicks it likes to play. Opportunity has a habit of slipping in through the back door, and sometimes it comes disguised in the form of misfortune or temporary defeat. Maybe that's why so many fail to recognize opportunity when it's right there in front of their face.

In the following chapters, my aim is to help you see prison in a different light. More than that, I intend to show you how you can apply the five Ps to your life right now instead of waiting on your release date to make some type of impact on the world and a solid change in your life. Still, I realize that not everyone is ready for change. No one can make another person ready. Have you ever tried to give advice to someone, and they weren't really trying to hear it? Or have you ever been offered good advice that you only now wished like hell you had listened to? Readiness comes in its own time (if at all). You've heard the saying, "You can lead a horse to water, but you can't make the motherfucker drink." If there is some small thirst, some openness to change and grow, as I assume there is since you picked up this book, your environment need not stop you.

So let's go!

Chapter 2

STATE OF MIND

So here you are, in prison. When you first entered this grim reality known as "The Yard," you learned real quick what the term "Total Institution" really meant. You were strip-searched with your ass cheeks spread, nut sack lifted, head shaved, property searched, and then you were assigned to living quarters. Before you got there, though, your first experience went down in a sociology or classification committee, where you were given a series of psychological and other test that evaluated you based on your personality, background, offense history, and treatment needs.

Being housed at an inaccessible prison, you found yourself physically cut off from your family, friends, and your former clique. If you were an active father, then you probably were depressed because you were anxious about your shorties. Your family might have found it difficult to travel way out to Bumfuck Egypt, right in the middle of nowhere, to come to visit you. Mail was censored and sometimes even destroyed. While the prison regulates what you wear, where you work, and sometimes even when you can sleep.

You have found yourself in an entirely new world with its own logic, behavior, rules, and language. It almost seems as if you have to adjust to and learn to live with the stress of prison life. By day you wait for count to clear for controlled movement—that once every few hours allows movement from one area of the prison to another. By night you sleep in an 8-by-12-foot cell, shacked up with someone you'd rather not even know. All the time, you are subject to the orders of COs who get on your everlasting nerves, not to mention the chaos and noise of hundreds of voices reverberating off steel and concrete walls. You realize that you have absolutely no privacy (even when racked up in your own cell), and since it is against the rules to cover your cell door with a towel, you find yourself constantly being watched by nosy, Peeping Tom onlookers. Let's not forget being woken up out of your good sleep due to a bright ass light beaming in your face, with a CO in front of your cell waiting on you to present your ID for roster count.

After maybe five-to-seven years in prison, you begin to see that many convicts live in prison-like, they're on a very long, fucked-up vacation, running low on cash and stuck in a cheap hotel. You notice that they pass the time doing little more than eating, sleeping, working out, watching TV, playing dominos, chess, and sometimes, by exception, knock or poker. Others may even spend their time hustling (Jags, Toon, Packs & Sacks) while trying to win the nearest mule. Eventually, you learn how to do time. This means slowing down, expecting little to jump-off. Both you and the COs are known to say, "You got nothing coming." This means that no one owes you a damn thing. Slow-motion is safer. Move fast, expect too much, and you might find yourself in a wreck.

So now consider a typical day in the pen. It may begin with the thought, "I need to get my ass up." And it's guaranteed to be followed by a succession of other thoughts, "What time is it? I wonder who's working the pod? Damn, I'm hungry. I should take my line down before I catch a case. I have to piss. Oh, snap, I forgot to send that letter out yesterday. I have to get that letter out today. I wonder who they're running for commissary? I hope my money hit. I hope I get some mail tonight. I need to check the scores to see if I hit the parlay." And on and on, an endless stream of constant thoughts and feelings running through the mind. Each taking its turn, hijacking your attention throughout the day until you go to sleep.

Most of us behind the wall can identify with these thoughts, feelings, and body sensations that are most intense at any given moment, even though they are only a small fragment of who we are. OR IS IT? The truth of the matter is that every man is what he is because of the thoughts that he allows to occupy his mind. As James Allen said, "Every man is what he thinks; his character being the complete sum of all his thoughts." If you wake up thinking about prison, then it's safe to say that over the years and through the course of your incarceration, you've become conditioned to step into that "Institutionalized" state of mind. Therefore, you are no longer "Free World," you are now penitentiary!

Any man who has conquered this weakness and has put away all evil, selfish, lazy, and unproductive thoughts belong neither to the warden or the state. He is free! The first thing you have to do in remaining free is to stay in control. No, you cannot control your environment. There is only one thing you can control—AND THAT IS A STATE OF MIND. A state of mind is something that you assume. You can't ask your family to mail it to you, and you can't blue-slip it from the commissary—it has to be created.

In creating a productive state of mind, it's crucial that you concentrate on your plans. Other than your safety, nothing else in your environment matters. Not even the fat booty CO who just stepped on the scene yelling "Female on the pod," because the time you put in planning for your release would accomplish miracles if it were concentrated on one thing. When you were a shorty, did you ever take a magnifying glass and let the sun's rays play through it on random objects? You know that as long as the rays were scattered all over the place, they pretty much did nothing. But focus the rays on one object and watch how quick something starts burning up. It's the same with your state of mind. You got to concentrate on one idea at a time with a burning desire.

But what is concentration? How do I learn how to concentrate, you might ask? Well, concentration is not something you learn how to do. It's something like Nike—YOU JUST DO IT! You concentrate whenever you get caught up in anything. Get so caught up in a Dallas Cowboys football game that when Ezekiel Elliott scores a rushing touchdown, you immediately jump up and down, not realizing you just knocked your cup of coffee over—THAT'S WHAT YOU CALL CONCENTRATION. Become so wrapped up in an episode of Empire that you don't realize it's count-time. You also don't realize that you are the only one standing there staring up at the TV while everyone else is staring at you, patiently waiting on you to fall inline so you can get counted—THAT'S CONCENTRATION!

And that's all concentration will ever be—getting so interested in one thing that you pay no attention to anything else that's going on around you. The biggest difference between those who succeed and those who fall

short at anything they attempt to put down is their level of commitment. Most people would love to be committed, but in practice, commitment requires an endless series of small painful acts. When a person has no way to deal with that pain, his commitment then comes to a standstill.
Concentration involves shutting out the rest of the prison world and focusing on one thing. For most people, that kind of effort is extremely painful.

So, is concentration and commitment just staring at the walls while daydreaming about what you're going to do once you touch down? No, it means that every act, every endeavor, and every attempt at anything you place effort and energy into is something predetermined for your post-release plan. For example, if you faithfully exercise with a rigorous workout regimen at least five times a week, your intention is not to look impressive so you can win a CO who can possibly smuggle drugs in for you.

On the other hand, your primary purpose for staying fit is so that you can practice the habit of maintaining a healthy lifestyle upon your release. With the state of mind that you have, you are on something new and smarter. Not the played out repetitious cycle that convicts been chasing for centuries.

If you listen closely to what most convicts are talking about in prison, you will realize that new ideas aren't even an option. Repetition is the hallmark of prison culture; it shuts out anything new. Just as old ways of thinking can trap one individual in a closed box, they can do that to an entire prison. It's happening to us right now. Life is passing us by while we continue with the same played out debates: Who's finer, Beyoncé or Rihanna? Who's richer, Jay or Dre? Who's the G.O.A.T., LeBron, or M.J.? Mixed with the same old prison gossip—I heard miss such-n- such has four kids...yeah, I also heard she fucks around with the captain.

The masses of our prison population are followers, not leaders— consumers, not producers—victims, not victors. Pay attention, and you will see that we're watching too much television, listening to too much radio, spending too much of our money on commissary, and wasting too much time. Don't get it twisted—this phenomenon is no accident. In a capitalist society, it's an absolute necessity to keep us chasing after kibbles and bits while being entertained is our number one focus. Those of you who are in this state of mind should be encouraged to know that the changing world that we are headed to is demanding new and smart methods of teaching, new and smart politics, new and smart technology, new and smart this, new and smart that. So tell me—how are we going to be effective when we get out of here with old and dumb ways of thinking? I advise you to change your state of mind, so you do not get left behind.

THE CONDITIONING OF THE MIND

We have billions of neurons in our brains and trillions of synapses that connect these neurons. Research has shown that we can train and develop our brains just like we can with our muscles. Our state of mind is the starting point for all habits and accomplishments. A state of mind that is easily distracted cannot see opportunities with clarity and urgency. What I suggest:

THE ISOLATION

> You have to leave the city of your comfort and go
>
> into the wilderness of your intuition. What you'll
>
> discover will be wonderful. What you'll discover
>
> will be yourself.
>
> —Alan Alda

When you're alone (especially in your cell) with your own thoughts, you begin to realize what your thoughts actually are. For some, this is a scary place. For me, it's electric. Do not allow your environment to distract you while creating a focused state of mind. One of the best ways to do that is disconnecting. Here's an exercise to practice:

1. Sit down and figure out what your biggest goal in life is.
2. Disconnect from the day-room for at least three in-and-outs.
3. Get rid of all your Jack Shots (and anything else that might distract you while you are in your cell)
4. Turn your radio off.
5. Think about exercise number one and make that goal the only thing you focus on.
6. Start setting it in motion.

I was able to accomplish great things while in prison, including my first book (Threat To The World), learning Spanish, and getting in the best shape of my life. Being disconnecting from the prison world helped me stay rooted in the present, which led to a laser-like concentration on my future goals.

Key Note: Spend time alone. Learn to be comfortable with your thoughts. Learn your thoughts, and you will create a better state of mind.

TITLES

Titles are great for music, movies, and books, but when used as a descriptor of a person, it's usually a euphemism for something either good or bad, like "Lazy" or "Focused." I know for a fact that I am far from being lazy, but I do apply the kind of focus to my work that most people apply to a game of chess. So here's an exercise for you. This is a list of titles. Circle the ones that you can personally identify with. Then determine what side of the fence illustrates a clear depiction of your general makeup. The side with the most circles wins.

GOOD

1) Established Author
2) College Student/Graduate
3) GED Student
4) Peer/Educator
5) Husband
6) Vegetarian
7) Physically Fit
8) Case Free
9) Smart
10) Nice
11) Inspiring
12) Loyal
13) Dedicated
14) Active Father
15) Positive
16) Humble
17) Leader
18) Avid Reader
19) Focused
20) Teacher

Number_____

BAD

1) Gangsta
2) Playa
3) Jack Artist / Monster
4) Gambler
5) Freestyler/Lier
6) Roach
7) Knock-Out Artist
8) Commissary King
9) Bad Actor
10) Kitchen Thief
11) Damn Fool
12) Bullshit Nigga
13) G4 Status
14) Lazy
15) Angry
16) Dope Fiend
17) Booty Bandit
18) Cell Warrior
19) Snitch
20) Loud

Number_____

Chapter 3

THE GAME IS OVER

That's right, I said it—THE GAME IS OVER! Still, I'm sensible enough to know that anyone who is in the game, representing the game or currently chasing the game, will not be trying to feel what I'm shooting at. Which is universally understood because I'm also realistic enough to know what kind of stain the game has on each of our hearts and brain. Likewise, I know the laws of loyalty, but the question is...DO YOU? The next time you put your headphones on, and you hear the song Loyalty by Kendrick Lamar (Featurng Rhihanna) come on the radio, listen to it with an open ear:

> Tell me who you loyal to
> Do it start with your woman
> or your man Do it end with
> your family and friends
> Are you loyal to yourself
> in advance
> I said tell me who you
> loyal to Is it anybody
> who you would lie for
> Anybody you would
> slide for Anybody you
> would die for
> That's what God's for

For far too long, we (the ones who's been out committing felonies) have been dedicated loyal soldiers to a game that draws zero interest. Even in here, we're still chasing a repetitive cycle that's getting us nowhere, like a rodent sprinting on a rat wheel. It doesn't stop cause the doors locked, right? Well, while you're standing there running in circles, ask yourself this: What's stopping you from applying that same loyalty to your children, your mother, or the female who's been devoutly and faithfully putting money into your account each and every month like clockwork?

Do you love knowing that your family is happy seeing you doing good? Well, there's a saying: Never do something that will jeopardize what you love doing the most. Me, myself I love my family, and I most definitely love winning, which is why I'm retired from the game...

BECAUSE I'M TIRED OF LOSING!

When we pull the curtain back and take a good look at the game that we've been chasing for centuries, we should have a telescopic view of what it actually is. I see a trap! Reason being why we "TRAP" because somehow, as human beings, we always instinctively call everything exactly what it is. Even the game itself. It should be centrally understood that when you play any game (no matter if it was a game of poker or Simon Says), eventually you lose. It's the fundamental laws of nature. What goes up must eventually come down.

Truth is, whatever game that you can possibly think of, in essence, all it is and all it will ever be is a gamble because there are no guarantees when you play games.

Question is, why do we continue to play Russian Roulette with our lives though?

Criminologists like to believe that the reason we commit crimes is that we have cognitive deficits and use information incorrectly when making critical decisions.

That we lack the ability to perform cognitive functions in normal and orderly fashions. That we are sensation seekers who are constantly looking for novel experiences, whereas we also lack deliberation and rarely think through problems and situations. That we have a different view of the world that shapes our thinking and colors our judgment. Because we have difficulty making the right decision while under stress, even while under confinement, we pursue behaviors that we perceive as beneficial and satisfying, but that, as a result, turn out to be harmful and detrimental. Not only to ourselves and everyone around us but also to our freedom.

The association between personality disorders and crime has a long history. In fact, several decades ago, psychologists linked personality to crime when they linked Antisocial Personality to crime. The APA (which is the Diagnostic and Statistical Manual of the American Psychiatric Association) defines Antisocial Personality as a pervasive pattern of disregard for, and violation of, the rights of others that begins early in childhood and continues into adulthood.

Individuals with this disorder may seem at first to be quite intelligent, charming, and highly persuasive. On closer examination, however, they often turn out to be manipulative and deceptive. In fact, some of the best con artists have antisocial personalities. They suggest that people suffering from this disease usually show the following behaviors:

- Failure to conform to social norms with respect to lawful behaviors as indicated by repeatedly performing acts that are grounds for arrest.

- Deceitfulness, as indicated by repeatedly lying, or conning others for personal profit or pleasure.

- Impulsivity or failure to plan ahead.

- Consistent irresponsibility, as indicated by repeated failure to sustain consistent work behavior or honor financial obligations.

- Lack of remorse, as indicated by being indifferent to or rationalizing having hurt, mistreated, or stolen from another.

Furthermore, criminologists and psychologists both link our criminal behavior to our environment, our upbringing, our experience, and even going to the extent to propose that the reason why we love the game and crime so much is because of the influence from violent music. Yeah, ok, but whether or not we have cognitive deficits, personality disorders, or listen to "Trap Music" (which is up for debate), it still does not subtract from my sentiment that the game itself is one big ass trap.

Michelle Alexander (legal scholar, professor, and author of The New Jim Crow) backs up my theory as she argues that racial castes in America has not ended—it was merely redesigned by targeting the hood through the war on drugs. By being confined to ghetto areas and lacking political powers, the black and poor are easy targets. Douglas Massy and Nancy Denton also explain in their book American Apartheid how racially segregated ghettos were deliberately created by federal policy, not impersonal market forces or private housing choices. The enduring racial isolation of the ghetto poor has made them uniquely vulnerable to the war on drugs.

The United States is and has been waging wars on multiple fronts.

Let's see—there are foreign wars like in Iraq and Afghanistan. Then there are the domestic battles the government is fighting at home against people like you and me, who use or sell drugs, pimp, panhandle, steal, con, rob, engage in the murder game, and join gangs. Ironically though, the war is titled "The War On Drugs," which was set in motion by President Nixon in 1970, intensified by President Reagan in 1980, and continues today unabated. After damn near 50 years and millions of arrests, there is no end because we continue to fall for the trap.

The war on drugs has provided the Criminal Justice System with crazy amounts of federal and state tax money to hire law enforcement, appoint judges, and build new jails and high-tech prisons. Too bad this tax money came from our people's paychecks and pockets. And another bad because the money was not spent on better schools, mass transit, and economic development that would create new jobs, as they were told.

William "Bill" Cooper in his book, Behold A Pale Horse, whistle-blowed the whole game by disclosing the fact that a hood near you was (and still are) under attack by the use of Silent Weapons For A Quiet War. He revealed a lengthy and detailed document that was dated 1979, but it outlines a policy that has been implemented since the 1950s.

The document says that: "The quiet war was...declared by the international elite at a meeting held in 1954." It says of the quiet war:

It shoots situations instead of bullets—propelled by data processing, instead of grains of gunpowder. Experience has proven that the simplest method of securing a silent weapon and gaining control of any inner city is to keep them undisciplined and ignorant of basic system principles on one the hand, while keeping them confused, disorganized, and distracted with matters of no real importance on the other hand. This is achieved by:

1. Disengaging their minds; sabotaging their mental activities; providing a low-quality program of public education in mathematics, system design and economics, and discouraging technical creativity by:

   a) Giving them what they desire—in excess—and depriving them of what they really need.

   b) Unrelenting emotional affrontations and attacks by way of the constant barrage of sex and violence.

2. Media: Keep their attention diverted away from real social issues and captivated by matters of no real importance.

3. Entertainment: Keep their entertainment below a sixth-grade level.

4. Schools: Keep them ignorant of real mathematics, real economics, real law, and real history.

My mission in no manner is to keep you updated on the latest conspiracy theories because when it's all said and done, we have at least the sound judgment and the power to distinguish right from wrong. But at the same time, it's also imperative that you understand the power of suggestion and how the system has been Pimp-N us since day one (and we thought WE were the one doing the Pimp-N). Some scholars have argued that the word "Penitentiary" may have been used first in connection with plans outlined in England in 1758 to house "Penitent Prostitutes."

Now, if that doesn't convince you that the powers-that-be consider us to be nothing more than a bunch of hoes, then I don't know what will. Wait, save the bar because I damn near forgot about free labor.

> "For private business, prison labor is like a pot of gold. No strikes. No union organizing. No health benefits, unemployment insurance, or worker's compensation to pay. No language barriers, as in foreign countries. New leviathan prisons are being built on thousands of eerie acres of factories inside the walls. Prisons do data entry for Chevron, make telephone reservations for TWA, raise hogs, shovel manure, and make circuit boards, limousines, waterbeds, and lingerie for Victoria's Secret; all at a fraction of the cost of free labor."
> Linda Evans and Eve Goldberg.

This cold reality harks all the way back to the days after the Civil War, when former slaves and their descendants were arrested for minor violations, slapped with heavy fines, and then tossed in a cage until they could pay their debts. The only means to pay off their debts was through labor on plantations and farms—known as convict leasing—or in prisons that had been converted to work farms. Paid next to nothing, convicts were effectively enslaved in perpetuity, as they were to earn enough to pay off their debts.

Sound familiar? Today, many convicts work in prison, typically earning far less than the minimum wage (often less than $3 per hour) sometimes as little as 25 cents. In the Great State of Texas, convicts work for free. Yet our accounts are "charged" for medical co-pays and other various expenses related to our incarceration (like court fees), making it seem damn near impossible to save our "Gifted Money" that would otherwise allow us to pay off our debt, plus help us make a successful transition when released from prison. Convicts in Texas are typically released with only the hand-me-down clothes on our backs with a complimentary $50 check.

The lack of pay in Texas prisons is first and foremost an issue of modern-day slavery and should be abolished for this reason alone. With an exception, there are convicts in here who, by all means, have to "get it how they live," which means they have to survive. Some hustle and traffic and trade within the system, so the slave labor trade that severely disadvantages those without outside support helps encourage prison violence. Placing convicts in an environment where we receive no compensation for work but are assessed fees for surviving is straight-up barbarous and inhumane on all levels. However, my fundamental premise for writing this book is not to fight or change the system (although the thought of us laying it down has crossed my mind once or twice).

Nevertheless, how I feel about that could be compared to how I feel about the game. I'm not in it, nor do I intend to be, so I "stay out the way" for those who are or want to be.

Likewise, for the lifers who have accepted prison as their fate and have come to realize that they will spend the rest of their natural lives here, I believe that working for free is their battle that they have to come to terms regarding whether they should accept it or not. Besides, I have come to understand fully that once the mind is conditioned to adapt and harmonize with working for free as their reality, there is hardly anything I or anyone else can do about it.

My main concern is "YOU," the one who is reading this book with the intention of making a successful transition when you touch down. At the same time, I did not write this book as food for you to digest and shit out like the slop we eat in the chow hall. Nor am I writing it so that you can follow me. I wrote it so that you, as a creator, can be inspired to move new and smart ideas forward in your own unique way. What I'm doing now is merely laying down the groundwork, which is a concrete example of what I consider to be a productive way of preparing yourself for the world. In no way am I saying that my way is the right way and the only way. As far as I know, we as humans tend to base our understanding about others and their motivations on what we think we know about ourselves and our own motivations. Then we decide that our way is both the "right" way and the "normal" way. All of us, to one degree or another, sometimes fall into the trap of assuming that everyone is supposed to "get like me."

However, as we move forward, my plan is to show you that our only limitations are the ones we set up in our own minds. Therefore, you can decide whether or not you want to try something different besides the common run-of-the-mill prison dialogue that you've heard daily.

From my own prison experience, I know that you hear the word "live" a lot. Ninety-nine times out of a hundred, the reason why convicts call anything at all "live" (especially to describe a particular prison facility) is because it's flooded with the game: cell phones, K-2, Reggie, and moving mules. Therefore, that particular unit is supposed to be considered as live. Well, I would like to paint a broader picture and contest that the only prison that is "live" is the one that has the highest parole rate. If you do not hear, "People are going home around here," then, in my opinion, that unit is not in any kind of way, form, or fashion…live. As far as the masses are concerned, the game is glorified, so you will hardly hear anything to the contrary.

No more effort is required to aim high in life and to demand success than is required to accept the loss. But what I want you to do is listen closely and pay attention before you fall victim to the conditioned state of mind that allows you to accept losing. Think about it—within your own prison experience, have you ever met someone in here who caught a cell phone case (which resulted in stacked time BTW) who didn't broadcast the fact that he got caught? That particular individual made it his duty to tell you (and anyone else for that matter) who was willing to listen. He sounds like 50 Cent, bragging about being shot nine times. It's a disturbing trend that's haunting prisons all over the U.S., and that trend is to make losing seem cool.

Despite having experienced these abnormalities and your prison record, overall, this is America, Jack—the land of second chances. Therefore, no matter who you are or what you have experienced in here, once you have completed your bid, you have the right to be free again.

So my sound, tight advice is to encourage you to hold on to your free world state of mind and to hold your head sky high, and to never accept the knock-off version of what convicts consider real.

IRON SHARPENS IRON

Essentially you should only associate with the convicts who place vice-grips on the type of traits and characteristics that complement the positive aspects of your own self-image. This type of positive energy and association will enhance your own development, and help confirm and establish the vision, emotions, and feelings you have about yourself. What I suggest:

STAND ON YOUR OWN TWO FEET

> In this world, where the game is played with
> loaded dice, a man must have a temper of
> iron, with armor proof to the blows of fate,
> and weapons to make his way against men.
> Life is one long battle; we have to fight at
> every step, and Voltaire very rightly says
> that if we succeed, it is at the point of
> the sword and that we die with the weapon in
> our hand.
> —Arthur Schopenhauer

One of the most difficult challenges you will face while here in prison is who you associate yourself with. I suggest that you make a conscious decision to stand on your own two feet and stay away from the negative crowd (especially the ones who are in the game). There are many unsuccessful, mediocre people all around you, ones who failed to recognize or act on their TRUE potential. If you constantly associate with them, your journey to greatness will be short-lived. Hustling for Nickle-and-Dimes is a contagious disease here in the pen, and if you're not careful, you will catch it.

Every day, each of us goes into battle either consciously or subconsciously. Every day I wage a ZERO TOLERANCE war on ignorance, and I make a conscious decision of who I build with. My everyday associations reflect my vision to relentlessly improve my mind, my body, and my soul. I write. I research. I study. I learn. I train. I practice. I develop.

I'm becoming stronger, smarter, and more enlightened through the commitment of my daily actions. Nothing (OR NO ONE) will derail me from my decision, commitment, and vision to improve myself.

Key Note: Declare war on who you associate with. Be relentless.

C ontinuously
R epeating
I diotic
M oves
E ffortlessly

L egal
E ndeavors
G et's
I t
T ogether

Using a Bureau of Justice Statistics, it shows that convicts released from state prisons have a five-year recidivism rate of 76.6%—the USSC (The Sentencing Commission) study calculated comparable federal prisoners related have a 44.7% re-arrest rate after five years.

The study included 1,048 prisoners who were older than 60 when released or paroled, over 4% of the total. Within six categories of prior criminal history, former convicts in the lowest level re-offended at a 30.2% rate, while those in the highest level were re-arrested at an 80% rate. The type of past offenses and the convict's education level were also included: Education level was as follows: 34.3% without a high school degree, 67.5% who completed a GED, 21.4% with some college, and 7.5% with a college degree.

Recidivism basically means being a repeat offender. Once you get accustomed to criminal activities in here (no matter if you are stealing blocks of cheese out of the kitchen and then selling it back on your wing), it will be difficult to shake the criminal addiction when you touch down. When things get tough, crime will always become an option for you, because legit money won't be fast and easy money. According to recidivism statistics, your best option is acquiring a college education while you have the opportunity…

THAT IS IF YOU WANT TO GET OUT AND STAY OUT!

Chapter 4

MASTER YOUR ENVIRONMENT

Some of the most well-known prison movies are: American Me, Blood In Blood Out, Cool Hand Luke and Escape From Alcatraz. It also bears mentioning that television programming has become increasingly saturated with images of prison. Some recent shows include the Netflix show Orange Is The New Black and the long-running HBO program OZ, which have managed to convince a lot of viewers that they know exactly what goes down in maximum security prisons.

But even those who do not consciously decide to watch a violent movie on the topic of prisons inevitably consume prison images, whether they want to or not, by the simple fact of hearing it. Nowadays, it is damn near impossible to avoid consuming images of prison life. Even you had an image of prison in your mind before you came here. Considering the fact that today there are more than two million Americans currently on lock-in correctional facilities, statistics say that nine times out of ten, you know of someone who came to prison before you hopped on that Blue Bird. A family member, someone on your old block, your baby momma's brother, or some old school in the county jail told you the stories. Likewise, somewhere down the line, you seen the pictures, the tattoos, the art, and you and I both know that you knew what "don't drop the soap" meant before you got here.

Now you are here to witness it firsthand. While living in this tight, controlled environment, far removed from what lies beyond those tall, razor-wired fences. But there's another side of the coin—something you may not realize even though you've been here now for X-amount of years. That this is an artificial world, with a very different social system than on the outside. Depending on how long you've been down, prison may have caused you to have little memory of something so simple as having an innocent conversation with an eight-year-old child. The longer you are on the inside, the more conditioned you become to the everyday prison routine. Making it more difficult for you to readjust to society.

Prison can affect you in more ways than just your

thinking—it can also affect the way you walk, the way you talk, and the way you eat. You will find yourself eating so fast as if you only have five minutes to swallow the whole damn tray. And unconsciously, you will get caught up in knocking on the table after you finish. Since our lives are so structured and almost entirely out of our control, we often suffer from an altered perception of time and an inability to put together a solid plan for our release. So it's like this—before you can focus on the "One Thing," first you have to master your environment. Like I said, you cannot in any way control your environment, but most definitely, you can master it. And that means learning from it and taking advantage of it. Pimp-N The Pen!

CREATURES OF HABIT

The first step in mastering your environment is, by all means, mastering your habits. Like prison, habits can make or break us to a far greater level than we would like to admit. Habits are both a powerful enemy and a wonderful team player to concentration. But you have to ditch the habits that are hazardous to your concentration and your post-release plan, and also embrace the ones that benefit it.

A large number of the prison population is controlled by our habits and are held in a chokehold by them, like a UFC fighter in the octagon. We do things in a certain way because of the power of habit. In no way does this mean that we've repeated a specific action enough times that it begins to look like instinct. It means that this behavior has become reinforced in our heads and in our bodies so much that it has become second nature, like that knocking on the table after you finish eating I mentioned.

Habits develop consistency. But consistency can either work in our favor or work against us. Repetition of bad habits kill our purpose and keeps us from reaching that next level of greatness. The convict who won't get any bigger goes out on the yard and constantly works out using the curl bar, but since his form is full of flaws and he won't allow his muscles to rest, he is not executing good habits. He thinks he's helping himself by putting in so much work on the yard, but he's actually hurting himself in the long run. All he's doing is reinforcing an incorrect workout that will eventually become second nature.

> "That's the problem with bad habits. They spread, they get magnified, eventually, they get noticed, like the convict who stepped out of his cell with his pants on backward."

You and I both know that convicts in here like to say "stay out of mine." Yeah, yeah, yeah, heard it a million times. For some odd reason, they suffer from the delusion that their intentions and thoughts can be kept on the low. Little do they know—they can't! They quickly develop into habits, and habits result into different circumstances.

Take, for example, sexual thoughts taking form into habits of public masturbation and sometimes even homosexuality, which results in circumstances of code 20s (sexual misconduct, disciplinary infractions) and disease. Lazy thoughts take form into habits of bad hygiene, pathological lying, and obesity, which result in circumstances of foulness, watching too much television and begging for soups (not to mention that shot of coffee that he has no intentions on paying back). Hateful thoughts take form into habits of fights and snitching, which result in circumstances of injury and loss of custody status.

On the other hand, good thoughts of all kinds take form into habits of peace and concentration, which result in better and brighter circumstances. Thoughts of courage, self-reliance, and decision-making take form into habits, which result in circumstances of success, physical fitness, respect, focus, greatness, and overall…YOUR FREEDOM!

Like I said, most of us are forming new habits all the time. But it's important that you remember the more you repeat something several times in the same way, the more you form the habit of doing it that exact way. The more you repeat it, the stronger that habit grows, and the more deeply it becomes rooted in your character. Don't play around with fire by forming bad habits, because as you know, bad habits are hard to break. So let's go ahead and identify these bad habits, so we can chop them down one at a time.

PUBLIC MASTURBATION

There are two types of people in this world. One type is known as leaders, and the other as followers. Take a few seconds and determine which one describes you. Keep in mind that if you have ever publicly masturbated on any female CO without her consent (and still continue this bad habit), then there's no way possible that you can be a leader. Because if you can't control yourself, then surely you can never control anyone else. Besides, the only reason anyone has ever done it in the first place is because they heard of someone else doing it. This clearly makes that individual a follower because you cannot begin to convince me that the average convict in here (who does that) was practicing exhibitionism before they drove up.

When we were amongst society, and if we would have so happened to stumble across a dude at Wal-Mart jacking off behind a clothes rack on a female who was peacefully minding her own business, you would have considered that shit insane. Do not lose your free world state of mind because guess what? IT STILL IS INSANE! The number one crime convicts love to hate the most is sex crimes. But little do the masses realize is that every time someone catches a code 20, the stronger the habit grows and the more deeply it becomes rooted in their character.

Accept it or not, but the more you play around with the "Jack Game," the more you are becoming a sex offender. Sex becomes your crime of choice. So if you are practicing this bad habit, kill it now because your dick can become a big distraction to your concentration. Your lower nature is weak, but you are strong. So control it, don't allow it to control you.

Transfer your sex energy

There are six primary forms of energy a man has in his life and he has to budget and channel this power effectively if he's ever going to accomplish the great goals he is capable of.

- Sexual Energy
- Physical Energy
- Psychological Energy
- Emotional Energy
- Social Energy
- Spiritual Energy

Guess which one holds the most weight?

Yup, you already know...sexual. Think of all the things men have done, created, destroyed, re-created throughout our history just to cut a Grade-A prime slice of what we consider a Bad Bitch. It's been said that all of our achievements have been to find a constructive outlet for sexual energy.

That's why you HAVE TO manage your sexual energy. Don't waste it on Jack Shots, Sub-0 Magazines, drowning your seed in the shower, or sniping a CO in the dark from the back of your cell. Instead, channel that energy into the creative force that it is. Don't cheat yourself, treat yourself of the ability to leverage that sexual potency.

I remember in the world when I was laying in my bed next to several fine works of art of women, post nut, and thinking, "For real, that was what I was in all that hurry to get...?" Five or maybe ten seconds of release? That's it? And all the effort before and during sex seemed almost frivolous when you're all done. Why not take some time to make something of the delightful pleasure? Re-direct your vital force, explore and enjoy the build-up of tension instead of running for the finish line. You'll start to appreciate the saying, "The point is not the destination; it's the journey."

Do you remember the movie Colors, when the old-school cop Uncle Bob Hodges (Robert Duvall) was narrating the joke about the two bulls to his partner Pac-Man (Sean Penn)? Well, if by chance you are either too young not to have seen the movie or just don't recall the joke, it went something like this:

One day a father bull and his son were standing on a grassy knoll, overlooking a herd of cows. Suddenly the son bull said to the father bull, "Hey, Pops, let's run down there and fuck one of those cows."

The father bull blankly stared at his son then said, "No, son, let's WALK down there and fuck them all."

The connotation of this joke is not implying to have multiple sex partners; it has a far deeper meaning. It suggests that all of us should take our time, pay attention and, therefore, reap the greater reward. The joke is the meaning of life!

Napoleon Hill, in his book, Think and Grow Rich, suggests that we should use sexual energy as a tool for transmutation. Sex transmutation simply means to switch the mind from thoughts of sex into something else creative, like say writing a book or an idea for success. In other words, embrace the sexual energy, but convert it. As quoted by Napoleon Hill:

The human mind responds to stimulation!

Among the greatest and most powerful of these stimuli is the urge of sex. When harnessed and transmuted, this driving force is capable of lifting men into that higher sphere of thought, which enables them to master the sources of worry and petty annoyance, which beset their pathway on the lower plane.

Man attains to the status of a genius ONLY when, and IF, he stimulates his mind so that it draws upon the forces available, through the creative faculty of the imagination. Chief among the stimuli with which this "stepping up" of the vibrations may be produced is sex energy.

The mere possession of this energy is not sufficient to produce a genius.

The energy must be transmuted from desire and action before it will lift one to the status of agenius.

Far from becoming geniuses, because of great sex desires, the majority of men lower themselves, through misunderstanding and misuse of this great force, to the status of the lower animals…

Note: Please excuse me for going hard on this particular subject, but some of these habits demand casting a little more light on than others.

COMPLAINING

We know all too well the convict who is always complaining about this or that: the food is trash, the dorms always get to go to chow first, they don't have shit on commissary, my celly is always in the cell, etc.
Nothing is ever right—you know the type.

As natural as this reaction seems, it's actually throwed off. You're refusing to accept an event that's already gone down. Nothing is a bigger waste of time. The more you complain, the more stuck you become. There's a common term for someone who lets himself roll around in misery and pain like this: A VICTIM! A victim thinks he knows how everything should operate. When people don't treat him the way he "deserves," he claims the whole system is against him. This becomes his rationale for giving up and falling back into his comfort zone, where he can stop trying. Inner strength comes only to those who move forward in the face of distress. But that's impossible for a victim who complains all the time.
His energy is wasted on thinking that it shouldn't have happened in the first place. He can't get that energy back until he accepts what went down.

Therefore, spend more time "DOING" and less time complaining.

GOSSIP

There is a saying: Rich people talk about plans and ideas, while poor people talk about things and other people. Gossip is a common practice in virtually every penitentiary there is, and it's not only "girlish," but it's also a big waste of time. Wasting too much energy on things that you cannot control, whether it's being envious of a convict (nine times out of ten), the one who is constantly on the phone, busting $95s, with two lbs of starch creased in his tight-whites, or being critical about him. Regardless if you believe it to be right or wrong, there is absolutely nothing you can do about it. Especially talking behind his back!

Do you know how many kids a certain CO has? Who she's fucking, who she's dropping-off to, etc.? Are you on top of the latest gossip? If so, ask yourself this: How am I going to use this information when I touch down? Gossip is defined as idle talk (WORTHLESS INFORMATION) about others. On top of that, gossiping is a cowardly act when you are talking about someone behind their back. But seeing how practically everyone does it (and it's common as the common cold) somehow makes it normal. Well, it is not normal because it is a counterpart of complaining. A big waste of time and energy!

Be rich and talk about plans and ideas, not other people.

SWEATING THINGS

I have a small brown plastic cup that a friend of mine gave me a couple years back. The cup is very small in stature, maybe half the size of an insert cup. It has no value—whatsoever—except maybe sentimental, because like I said, a friend of mine gave it to me. The crazy thing is, this small little brown plastic cup attracts a lot of attention. Some people have even made attempts to pick it up and admire it. Well, you know that didn't happen! But why do you think this cup (that holds no weight) attracts so much attention? That's right, simply because it's different from the regular bulky green cups that are currently floating around.

Some convicts have a bad habit of noticing, admiring, and cherishing "THINGS" that are different but ridiculing different personalities, and those who have what is called a distinctive state of mind. This bad habit allows you to conform to the norm and, therefore, catch the virus of sweating things that hold absolutely no weight.

Do you get nervous knowing that shake-down is approaching? When you start hearing the rumors being tossed around in the air about lock-down, do you feel anxiety or start stressing about your property? Granted, I know that all of our earthly possessions can only fit in three (maybe four) commissary mesh bags, but seeing that you are trying to go home (obviously, you don't have any contraband) there's nothing to sweat.

Everything that you own can be purchased at the nearest Family Dollar, so I know you don't intend to take any of that shit with you. For this reason alone, let it go if the threat ever pops up, and your property isn't legit. Do not get caught up in the habit of sweating "THINGS" because every little plastic item that we own in here is replaceable, but your state of mind is priceless.

ANGER

Developing the habit of being angry all the time is a clear sign of weakness, so don't get it confused with strength. Anyone who loses his temper all the time automatically places himself at a disadvantage.

Muhammad Ali's tactic was simple—whoever he wanted to defeat, first, he made them angry. Under the influence of anger, a convict does all kinds of unbalanced things that he'll later regret. He throws temper tantrums and acts like an out of control child.

Anger is like a madness phase of insanity when it's not in check. Look around for yourself. The next angry convict you run across (believe me, they're not hard to find in prison) look into his eyes and see how much he reminds you of a maniac.

It's a well-known fact that if you can keep your cool while you've been challenged mentally or physically and your opponent is in rage, you have the upper hand because you are the one dealing with an irrational one. It's better to fall back and allow the other one to pound his fist against his chest in his own anger while you're staying cool and solid. Besides, it's easy to cool down an angry person without becoming angry yourself because, as you know—it takes two to tango.

You will find that if you are able to control your voice, keeping it steady, cool, calm, and collected at a low-pitch, you will not fly into his craziness. You will find by doing that, the voice of the other convict will gradually turn down a few notches from his loud, roaring tone, and before you know it, both of you will be pitching your voice to the same key that you set the tone too.

If you find yourself angry daily, try to kill this bad habit ASAP because I cannot stress enough how weak it is. You do not want to be released back into society with the mind frame of an unbalanced maniac.
You wouldn't even be able to drive a vehicle without becoming subject to road rage. Which is an easy ticket back to prison and also leads to death! I have heard countless stories about convicts getting out and, as a result, getting their wigs split due to unnecessary aggression.

WARNING! Keep in mind, people do not fight in the world...
THEY SHOOT!!!

WASTING TIME

Believe it or not, but the time that we have on our hands is our most valuable asset. Put it like this, if the old cliché "Time Is Money" were actually true, then we would all be labeled as millionaires. Actually, the time that we have has a far greater monetary value than money. Seeing as how money (no matter if it were one dollar or a million dollars) could be replaced.

Time, on the other hand, cannot be replaced—likewise, it cannot be reimbursed or repeated either. So in a sense, time is priceless, right?

Kill the habit of wasting time because how you spend your hours, days, weeks, years will determine the level of success you will experience when you touch down.

QUESTION: If you were to win a million-dollar lottery ticket, what would you do with the money? I hope you said INVEST IT! Because a better way to look at how to allocate your time is to speak in terms of investing it, rather than spending or wasting it. To spend has an indication of finality, with no return (IT'S A WRAP). To waste? Well, that simply means that you ran through it on meaningless, insignificant shit. Might as well flush it down the damn toilet…BECAUSE YOU HAVE NOTHING TO SHOW FOR IT!

Invest our time by …

MAKE A ROUTINE

You are no stranger to this because convicts live and die by what we call our "Routine." A routine is simply a daily list of activities we follow each and every day precisely all the way down to the minute. You wake up every day at the same time, you wait for in-and-out at the same time, you expect to be counted every day at the same time, and you go to sleep every night at the same time.
Meanwhile, you eat the same food, wear the same clothes, you see the same people and the same c.o's.

Everything you see is basically gray and white, and you have no physical freedom every day at the exact same time.

However, to have a PRODUCTIVE routine means that every minute and everyday counts. I learned how to use this prison routine to my advantage by relentlessly scheduling every minute of my days.

For example:

* I know that the first drop for the dayroom is at 6:00am. Therefore, I will set my alarm clock for 4:00am, giving me a two-hour window of opportunity to study for college exams.

* TDC jobs pay $0.00 per hour. Insomuch as to why I do not get caught up in the "Good Job" syndrome. The best jobs in the world are the ones that pay the most. In here, the best job (FOR ME) is the one with the least amount of hours (which is breakfast shift kitchen: 2-3 hrs. max), giving me more time to write this book.

What I suggest:

Ask yourself "What's is the best use of my time right now?" Then act accordingly. To take advantage of your time means that your biggest investment is in YOURSELF.

HOW MUCH ARE YOU WORTH?

Fill in the blank:

I am worth $ _____ dollars.

This question is not characterized by mere conventional virtues. I do not care how trustworthy, nice, loyal, or honorable you are. This is a business question. So if I were an investor (and I was looking to invest money in something or someone), what do you have, know, or can do that will convince me to invest the above amount of money on you?

Key Note: Know your worth, and by the time you get out of here, make sure you know for damn sure you are worth every penny of it.

FAILURE TO COMMUNICATE

It's common for convicts who have very little knowledge to try to give the impression that they have a lot of it. People like this generally have the habit of talking too much and listening very little. Keep your eyes and ears wide open, and your mouth closed. Those who talk too much do little of everything else. If you have the habit of talking more than you're listening, you're not only depriving yourself of many opportunities to soak up useful knowledge, but you're also revealing your hand to people who are sitting back in the cut just waiting to defeat you.

We also know the convict who has to win every conversation and every debate. They are the ones who are forever talking both the loudest and the longest without giving you any airtime (as if every conversation has a winner and a loser). A failure to communicate is when someone is telling you their life story, but you are constantly cutting them off in the middle of their story with a long and drawn-out fairy tale about yours.

If you have the habit of always wanting to be right, then you will never be a good communicator. Winning debates and conversations is not what's up. We as convicts have to do better at communicating because communicating is a habit just like the other ones we've talked about. And being a habit, like your environment, it can be learned and mastered. It is an important habit, so instead of ditching it, make it good because it deserves its own 1, 2, 3 steps, and its own place on the path to your success. For "Communication Rules The Nation" is not just a saying—it's a fact!

DOPE FIEND MENTALITY

A lot of convicts think they kicked their habit in the pen, only to return to the streets and get perpetually addicted again. It's rare, but a select few in here realize the importance of identifying and mastering substance abuse before they return to a free world of unlimited strip clubs, homies with sacks, and Bad Bitches who love to party. It's too easy to get sucked right back into the old dope fiend mentalities that we are all familiar with.

If you have ever taken the classes Changes or Cognitive Intervention, then it's a big possibility that you've seen the documentary, Omar & Pete. As you know, initially, the film was supposed to be about Omar, the devout Muslim who had big aspirations to start his own business (in fact, he did).

But unfortunately, left out of calculation was his drug addiction.

Omar mastered everything except his number one kryptonite: his dope fiend mentality! Too bad, we had to witness his downfall, but without warning, Pete, who was not in the cards, taught us all a valuable lesson. In order to stay out and be successful, first, you have to identify with and master your dope fiend mentality.

Let's break down the terminology of how we use the word dope fiend anyway. We see them all the time on the block. We have served them plenty of times too. Some are loyal customers than others, but whenever you had good work, most definitely, you could count on a dope fiend to make ends meet. They brought you merchandise too—say a brand new PlayStation for the black market (sticker price) of maybe three dime rocks. Every now and then, they showed up with a 60-inch plasma, sometimes designer bags for your girl, and, on occasion, school uniforms for the kids. Reason being because most dope fiends commit crimes solely to buy drugs. Females even go to the extent of prostituting for it. I don't know about you, but quite a few times, the thought ran through my mind: "if dope fiends didn't do drugs, they could actually be rich because they never run out of unique ways nor the ambition to purchase and smoke work."

If you have the habit of doing drugs while down here in the pen, is it safe to say that YOU TOO have a dope fiend mentality? All of your efforts and all of your best game was put down exclusively to get high.

Regardless, if you smoke reggie, bug out on toon, snort pills in the dayroom, or drink hooch on the regular, your primary goal is to stay lit. Instead of discarding your habit, you are now multiplying it by 10.

Imagine what kind of fascinating things you could accomplish just by converting that energy into the "One Thing." Don't allow your true character to be rooted into a dope fiend. You are a Boss! Bosses do great things, nothing average.

Think of the richest person that you could possibly think of. Got him? Ok, now could you imagine that same person living within your living quarters smoking drugs, snorting pills, or so drunk from hooch that you would have to escort him to his cell? Thought not! Because to be rich you have to THINK MONEY- NOT DOPE! Remember, you are the complete sum of all your thoughts. So if you have the habit of thinking about getting high majority of the time, do not refer to yourself as "live" or "turnt-up." Instead, tell the truth and admit that you have what we are all familiar with...A DOPE FIEND MENTALITY.

THIS SHIT RIGHT HERRRE NIGGA!

K2 is a physical drug with heroin-like addictions—therefore, it causes your body to NEED it, which is why most people have an increased desire to get high. As a result, K2 can cause multiple seizures, kidney failure, along with massive heart attacks because it reduces blood flow to the heart. In addition, K2 can cause an unfathomed number of catastrophic events to the body, with brain damage and paralysis to add to that list. Not to mention, it's manufactured with a toxic poison labeled as JWH-018 with a cocktail of other life-threatening chemicals (sometimes rat poison and roach spray) like MDPD, which is: Methylenedioxypyrovalerone, Mephedrone and Methylene.

WTF? So you mean to tell me that convicts are willing to smoke something that can cause DEATH? This shit right herrre nigga!

YOUR LIFE LINE

Dependency is the inability to act independently, which in truth is the cold reality of doing time. We depend on someone else for a number of reasons: to run chow, to open our celldoors, we depend on someone for a channel check, someone to sign our slips so we can go to the commissary. More than that—we depend on someone from the outside to send us the money...on and on, and the list goes on. But I think the name of the game is to minimize our dependency, so we don't get accustomed to someone else holding our hands and carrying our weight throughout life. Especially if it's within our control.

Do you realize that the phones (that the State of Texas has finally provided for us) are our lifelines? It's one of my prime resources for having the ability to write this book, it's how I am a factor in my children's lives, it's how I receive and give positive energy to my family. How are you using the phone? Do you have a bad habit of asking your family to call down here for any and everything under the sun? Have you ever asked them to call down here because:

1) An officer working the pod didn't do an In-And-Out on time.
2) They skipped your building on commissary.
3) It's been two days, and you still haven't been called for your eComm.
4) The food is cold in the chow hall.
5) They served pancakes for a week straight.
6) An officer confiscated your cup (that you left unattended on the front bench) when you went to chow.
7) You and your celly ain't clickin so "ALL OF A SUDDEN" now you want to get moved.
8) It's been a week, and you still haven't received your KITE magazine.
9) It's 9:00 PM, and they still haven't passed out the mail. Oh, and I love this one:
10) You had your loved one call the warden because you were written up for something that you know damn well you were guilty of.

Don't get it twisted because I know that some of these COs are not exempt from writing bogus cases. But when it's all said and done, we have to MAN UP! Stop having your family call down here for frivolous reasons. Because there's going to be a time that you are going to REALLY need someone to call down here for an emergency—but guess what? You've already burned up your lifeline.

Remember what I said about the victim. Also, read the Baby Boy Syndrome in the book How To Hustle And Win.

Use your lifeline wisely. It's how you stay connected, it's how you stay free world, it's how you vanish from the prison world for at least 30 minutes. Do not waste your lifeline by Googling someone's charge. **WHAT THE FUCK DOES IT MATTER IF SOMEONE HAS A SEX CHARGE?** How are you going to

use that information when you touch down? If you are that concerned about someone's charge (that you deemed it necessary to ask your people to look them up), then maybe you should convert that energy into getting out of here. That way, you can protect YOUR OWN CHILDREN away from perverted and wicked people. Besides, there are several other things you can do with your lifeline other than being nosy.

Develop positive habits and express good energy when talking to your love ones. In doing so, try your hardest to refrain from using the two words "can you" followed by a bunch or unnecessary bullshit.

ENTERTAINMENT

If you have to habit of...hold up—my bad. This subject deserves its own chapter because entertainment is by far our most vigorous habit and the number one distraction to our concentration. So let's break it all the way down to its roots.

However, before we get to the ENTERTAINMENT chapter, here's a list of additional habits that you should try your hardest to eliminate. I thought about these habits after one of my college instructors proposed that for the average incarcerated man in America, his mind capacity reduces to 14 years old.

1. Lazy! Stop the habit of being lazy because a 14-year-old child has zero sense of responsibility. Which explains why he has no problem staying glued to a video game or television set all day if his parents allowed him to.
2. Kill the habit of eating anything and everything. Establish better eating habits because a 14-year-old child has no conscience at all about what he decides to place into his body. The next time they run commissary on your building, pay attention!
3. Stop the habit of "CLOWNING" in the education dept. You are not a class clown, nor are you 14 years old. You are a GROWN ASS MAN (A BOSS AT THAT) So stop playing and learn something. It should not take you two years to get a GED.
4. Stop the habit of trying to be overly hard. This is not the 90s era—this is a new millennium where you have to use your BRAIN to survive. So kill the animation and stop trying to sell a wolf ticket. A 14-year-old child has everything to prove, NOTHING TO GAIN!
5. Stop the habit of scorin (or high-sidin) on your fellow convicts. A 14-year-old child has telescopic eyesight for physical flaws but fails to recognize anyone's distinctive personality characteristics.
6. Stop the habit of taking ownership of things that do not belong to you: benches, tables, phones, cells, TVs, etc. A 14-year-old child will be willing to go to war (even with his sibling) for the shotgun seat of his mother's car.

Like I said, it's time to **MAN UP**! We are grown men, and we have children to raise once we are released from this institutional playground. Therefore, make grown man decisions.

Chapter 5

THE BREAD AND CIRCUSES

I don't know if you know or not but it would be my pleasure to lace you up to the fact that the phrase "Bread and Circus" has become an all too familiar place to describe how the Roman Empire managed to keep the masses controlled and satisfied during the long centuries of its decline. By providing enough food to keep their guts full and enough amusement to keep their minds entertained, the ruling classes were able to avoid social unrest. Back in the day of the Roman Empire, those were the keys to diverting the public's attention from political greed and corruption and particularly, from the massive gap between the rich and the poor.

Therefore, Julius Caesar said, "Give them bread and circuses."

It's no secret that after Rome won countless wars, it was overrun with captured slaves, and they performed the physical labor. Idle, unemployed Romans were restless. Julius Caesar perfected the ideal satisfaction: give them wheat to eat and violent entertainment to enjoy. Guess what? It worked!

Generally, the Plebeians neither starved nor rioted. Salivating, they would watch gladiators slaughter animals and each other. Those gladiators were mainly slaves, but as they won fights, they could win their freedom and rake in donations from the crowd. Who knows if this policy was consciously adopted, but its influence most definitely spread across the globe. It would not have been either the first or the last time that providing food and games to prevent a community from separating themselves from the iron fist of the law would be successful.

In the Persian Wars, the first historian of the west, the Greek Herodotus, describes how Atys, king of Lydia in Asia Minor, introduced ball games some three thousand years ago as a way to distract his subjects when a series of bad crops caused unrest in the hungry populations.

The plan was to keep them engaged in games one day so much as not to feel any craving for food, and the next day to eat and abstain from games. This same pattern went down for like 18 years.

A similar pattern jumped off in Constantinople during the waning of the Byzantine Empire. To keep the citizens happy, great chariot races were held in the city. The best drivers became rich and famous, and they were automatically elected to the senate. Even in Central America before the Spanish conquest, the Mayas developed elaborate games something like basketball, which kept spectators busy for weeks on end. Likewise, you see it today in our country, where young black and brown people depend on sports and entertainment as avenues to social mobility: basketball, football, baseball, boxing, and rap careers absorb our youth's energy because it promises—you already know...wealth and fame!

It's no coincidence that sports itself is big business in this country. You have no other choice but to wonder if the same political strategy—Bread And Circuses—is at work right here in the United States to keep the people from reacting to ugly truths like the fact that 95% of the economic gains in recovery have gone to the richest 1%, and the majority of National Football League owners are billionaires but still get taxpayers to dish out 70 to 80% of the cost of new stadiums.

The professional sports leagues are joined at the hip with federal, state, and local governments. So, is it farfetched to put two and two together to get the idea that today's bread and circuses constitute a camouflaged politician/pro-league plan to pacify the everyday, working-class citizen? Is it over the top to be inclined to think that the United States is as bloodthirsty as ancient Rome?

Well, let's first take a look at Detroit. Right around the time, it became the nation's largest major city to go bankrupt, the state okayed a $650 million hockey arena for the Detroit Red Wings. Damn near half of the money came from taxpayers. The team owner is the Ilitch family of Little Caesars Pizza, which also owns the Detroit Tigers and a big chunk of a downtown gambling casino. Forbes magazine says the Ilitch family is worth around $3.2 billion.

Early in the Detroit bankruptcy, there jumped off a battle that might have made even Julius Caesar's eyebrows raise. The Detroit Institute of Arts houses city-owned art worth $421 million to $805 million (it also holds many other pieces owned by individuals). These city-owned pieces are works by great artists: Bruegel The Elder, Degas, Van Gogh, Matisse. The city's emergency manager hired charities to appraise the art, with the idea it could be sold to help rescue the city (the institute and several foundations are attempting to raise hundreds of millions to rescue this art museum), but this is still a dry run. Creditors claim the art is undervalued. Other stumbling blocks remain.

Yeah, but guess what? There were no stumbling blocks for the hockey arena and the gladiators who will get it in and check paper with hard blows to each other's head. Yet that large ass subsidy is still going forward right now as you read this book.

We all remember August of 2005 when Hurricane Katrina devastated New Orleans. Thousands of people were stranded—almost 2,000 died. But did you know what was one of the first orders of business? That's right—the Superdome, where the New Orleans Saints play, was completely put back into shape. The cost was $336 million—$156 million from the FEMA (Federal Emergency Management Agency) and another $121 million from the state. The 2013 Super Bowl was played there. It is hailed as a great rescue operation while "the hood" continue to wither and die.

The indoor stadium is now called the Mercedes Benz Superdome. And the Saints' owner is no less than a billionaire.

Bottom line: Team owners and federal, state, and local governments work together to provide the violence- seated circuses.

HAIL TO MOTHERFUCKING CAESAR

The Oxford Reference provides the following definition for bread and circuses: A term referring to the potential of spectator sports and mass spectacle to divert populations or fractions of a population away from the weightier business of politics and society.

Now the question is, can you find any similarities between our artificial prison world of the Roman Empire and those of the "Bread and Circuses" during the years like sports in the United States? That should be easy considering that entertainment is our number one focus (not to mention, our number one habit that distracts our concentration). There are entire penitentiaries (including yours) where you automatically receive the impression from talking even with convicts who live within your living quarters besides commissary, TV, rec, games, "the game," sports, and gossip, there is not that much else that captures our attention.

Well, with the exception of religion, but from my supposition, religion has been used mainly as a tool to CONTROL and SEPARATE us just as it's been adapted to CONTROL and SEPARATE entire nations. Me personally, all I would like to do is believe in God, not hate or judge someone else for not worshiping Him in the same allegiance as I do.

Anyway, back to the matter at hand, because as you know, when Sunday falls around the matter for discussion is not (for the most part) God the Father. You know just as well as I do that the NFL has the largest turnout.

Convicts gather around the benches in droves, some even sitting on the floor as the TV draws a massive crowd. Every Sunday like clockwork: parlays, pick-ems, shot-gun boards, fantasy football, and master sheets flow through circulation as if they were in Vegas with real money at stake.

Like I said earlier, this is no mistake. Even the system here is designed to keep you chasing after kibbles and bits while being entertained. As long as (the masses) prison population's attention is diverted away from real controversial issues (like free labor or failed policies, then everything is cool. Then we have the nerve to *not even question* why we live in an establishment where we are provided with brand new plasma flatscreen televisions (and numerous cable channels to select from) but are yet to receive air-conditioning. Believe me, you are not an imminent threat to the system or its agenda by knowing LeBron's stats, nor will that information help or assist you in the least toward your post-release plan.

What about commissary? Is that considered as entertainment too? Well, convicts serving time in Texas' prisons can buy certain "free world" goods: snacks, clothes, even cosmetics—provided that our people on the outside send us the money.

It's a bustling business. During the last fiscal year, convicts spent about $95 million on commissary (not including ecomm). The most popular purchases? We bought $18 million in chips and snacks, as the department categorizes them, during the fiscal year 2017. We spent another $15 million on assorted drinks, including 3.5 million cans of Coca-Cola.

Ramen noodles are staples. The Texas Prison System sold a whopping 33 million 30-cent packages during that period.

The cost: $9.9 million and another $9.4 million on meat products, prison records show. The sales data, obtained under the Texas Public Information Act, offer a shocking glimpse of our prison life, our spending habits, and how much of our money we are contributing to The Beast.

There's a certain kind of status that comes with having the ability to go to commissary.

Reason being that not everyone has that same privilege. So, in essence, it becomes a source of pride. A bragging right that says, "I have money!"

Well, let me lace you up on a well-known fact— COMMISSARY IS NOT MONEY. IT'S FOOD! (junk food at that) and that's all it will ever be.

Peep game, say for instance your family fell off, and consequently, all you have to your name is the $300 that you have on your account. Not thinking of investing or save it, you go to the commissary three times within a two months time span and exchange the $300 into food items: Coffee, chips, meat packs, Zoo-Zoo & Wham-Whams, etc. Now out of the blue, a lawyer contacts you, reassuring you that he can get your case overturned, and all he's asking to represent you is a $300 down payment. He said that you could pay him the remaining balance upon your release. Question: do you honestly believe that you could pay the attorney with the $300 worth of commissary that you have hoarded in your locker? No, because you come to realize that commissary is not money. The only thing you can do with it is eating it and shit it out, and therefore, it no longer exists anymore.

Granted, I know that commissary has a prison commerce value that gives you a license to traffic & trade within the system. Guess what? That's where all of your negotiations, business endeavors, and your best wheeling and dealing will ever stay: "within the system" as long as your mind is there too. Once you start thinking "free world," you will begin to appreciate those numbers on your account and get more satisfaction from seeing the numbers increase instead of decrease.

This bread and circus mentality has spread throughout the entire U.S prison system like the Covid-19 virus, and it seems to have no prevalent cure. The masses have accepted this altered state of reality, which can also be observed with the same concepts of diversion methods in antiquity.

Just like ancient Rome, the prison system uses reverse psychology tactics in convincing us that going to commissary and being glued to a television set all damn day is supposed to be some type of privilege. Well, do you really believe that if we suddenly stopped wasting all our money on commissary and pulled up from the televisions that everything would be fine-and-dandy? Hell no! They will be coming in your living quarters with thorough investigations, trying to figure out what in the hell is going on.

I encourage you to stop the habit of wasting your time and money on junk food and entertainment because it has no monetary value whatsoever. However, there is nothing wrong with going to the store and watching a little television every now and then, but do not let the dosage prevail over your plans. Because when you break it all the way down to its lowest common denominator—You are a Boss and I know for damn sure that you are not a clown in nobody's circus.

Because with your free world state of mind, you will never be caught dead in the 100° weather, on the side of the highway with a sign held over your head that says: WILL HUSTLE FOR FOOD!

SLAVES TO THE DEVILS

Sitting contemplating the manipulation of our current generation

No general leader, evil seekers intend to decrease our motivation

The whole nation contents

Bent, under a spell, "HELL" driven suicide

Genocide endeavors ....Recognize

Aids was created to depopulize
Media? Television? ....Hypnotize
Keep our attention diverted away from real social issues
Continue the drama with silent weapons aimed at me and you Bitch niggas can't peep the simplest of methods

Giving us what we desire -Hire- fake rappers that fed it Trap stars, slab cars, ice chains, designer clothes, dame hoes Et Cetera - Et Cetera

Entertainment has us trapped in a web of a sixth-grade level Shovels handed to us to dig our own graves

SLAVES TO THE DEVILS

Disengage our minds, sabotaging our mental activities Providing a low-quality education -Stimulating- with constant drama, gossip What happen to creativity

Mentally we are dying, I'm silently crying, trying my hardest But it seems that we are the farthest

From waking up to a full cup that we were given Yet remain thirsty to objectives that was hidden

It's sad but I guess we will remain on a sixth-grade level Shovels handed to us to dig our own graves

SLAVES TO THE DEVILS

Poem written by: Richard Spraggins

Chapter 6

COLOR BLIND

There is nothing more powerful than a human mind determined to think and act for itself. Such a phenomenon is a manipulator's nightmare, and, like everyone behind the wall, you have that power. You have that power to refuse the racism trend that is currently haunting Texas prisons. Do not doubt for one second that the administration doesn't know that we are segregated. Trust me, they know that the benches are divided along racial and gang-related seat arrangements. Which is frivolous because the majority of the time, this is only happening on minimum and medium security units. WITH NOTHING GOING ON! That's why I call it a trend because followers are the only group of people who abide by that shit.

Don't get it twisted because the administration loves to see blacks, whites, Mexicans, and Asians separated. Because when we're separated, they (the administration) can't harness the incredible power that we possess collectively. The power we would have if we build together.
The power we would have it we made money together, supported each other, and at the beginning and end of each day, STAYED TOGETHER.

Convicts need to start realizing that we're all fighting the same battle. It's not a battle of black against white or Fama against Tango Blast or Crip against Blood. Nor is it a battle of D-Town against H-Town. It's a battle against a lack of education. A battle against a lack of positive energy. A battle against idle time. A battle against a lack of vision, a lack of creativity, a lack of motivation, and a lack of diversity. We're all fighting the exact same battle.

No matter what your motivation is, I'm glad you're here because I'm trying to speak to everyone who can hear me.

Regardless of your race or affiliation, feel me? No doubt, if you try to speak to everyone at once, sometimes you just end up making a lot of white noise. But I'm someone who's always tried to connect with as many people as possible. I want to be able to build with the white dudes in the dorms just like I chop it up with the gangstas in the buildings. That's how you learn to network.

And that is the developing of contacts of exchanging of information to further one's cause. A skill that I advise you to master before you get out of here because you never know what kind of doors could possibly open if you would just become color blind.

No one can follow it down through the ages without realizing that the whole purpose of existence is growth. In all nature, to cease to grow is to die. That's why you can't let negativity get in your ear. Your ear is like an embryo—negative ideas will grow in there if you're not careful, and then you become the one who ceases to grow and develop. You become stuck in ancient times, not realizing that racism (especially individual discrimination) is played out.

However, Institutional Discrimination is an entirely different beast. So in the next chapter, I will demonstrate how we (as black people) have the power to either accept or kill what has been predetermined for us to do and act for at least 300 hundred years (from the date it was predicted). Also, I do not deny the fact that there are "traps" laid out for us, but as of today, these traps are color blind. "The Beast" does not discriminate! Have your people send you the Meth Epidemic In America and decide for yourself what race it predominately affects. Yeah, individual discrimination is trying to resurface in the world, but if you ask me, it's just a bunch of insignificant propaganda. Mostly coming from little ignorant ass millennials who haven't the slightest clue of what racism really is.

For instance, many people condemn Colin Kaepernick and those who kneeled during the National Anthem as disrespectful to veterans who fought and died for this country, yet support those who display the flag of a sworn enemy. Too many people fly the confederate battle flag with pride, even though it represents a country that killed many union soldiers. Now, if that's not disrespectful to soldiers who gave their lives on this soil to preserve the United States of America, then please tell me what is? That's why I advise you not to get caught up in it because nine times out of 10, a racist person is uneducated and therefore has no justifiable grounds for having this big chip on their shoulder because of someone else's skin color.

Taking an interest in others despite their race is an art that has to be mastered right now before you touch down. If you will chill for a minute or two and think, you will find that the people whose personality seems the most attractive to you are the people who seem to take an interest in your own personality. The people who navigate towards you, are they putting you on with solid advice? Are they doing positive things and utilizing their time wisely? What projects are they working on? Are they attending college classes? Are they making progressive efforts to be a part of their children's lives? What about their conversations? Is the majority of what they're talking about free-world plans or penitentiary fantasies? Taking a look at who you surround yourself with is taking a good look at yourself, because as you know, birds of a feather, flock together. If you hang with ignorant people then you're bound to become ignorant yourself. Yeah, because as things go, ignorance is color blind too.

Chapter 7

STUCK IN A TIME WARP

As I pointed out in Chapter 2, America is demanding new and smart methods of everything, from technology to new and smart methods of teaching children how to apply critical thinking to their education. In short, we are headed to an advanced world with improvements basically on everything that you can possibly imagine. So what you learned how to operate the latest iPhone inside your cell—it still does not mean that you have everything else figured out. There are eight-year-old kids out there who can not only operate an iPhone but add apps, write code, and hack someone else's iPhone too. The world is advancing at economical speed while we're down here stuck in ancient times. As a felon, all the odds are stacked highly against us—therefore, in order to compete in this advanced world, it's important for us to cultivate our thinking to the rate of its progress, not centering our attention on matters that have zero relevance whatsoever.

Let me paint a picture for you. If you're an old head like me, then nine times out of ten, you recall the movie I'm Gonna Git You Sucka. Well, you saw for yourself how the throw-back pimp, Suga Bear got out of the pen after maybe a couple of decades. He stepped out wearing a Dutch pink, yellow suit with butterfly collars, a humongous boater-style hat, six-inch (FISH TANK) platform shoes, with the Gangsta-Pimp walk to match. You could not have told him he wasn't doing his best shit. But when the laughs, rocks, and reality struck, he came to the realization that he looked like a goddamn clown.
Unfortunately for Suga Bear, but he was stuck in a time warp!

So many of us are stuck in a time warp as well, but the sad part of the game is that some (or should I say most of us) don't even know it.

Prime reason why I can't cut any corners with this subject. Reason being why I have to be blunt and straight to the point. WARNING! If you're not prepared and ALL THE WAY DOWN to face the facts, then you might want to skip this chapter because I'm going to hit you in the jugular vein. Are you ready? Ok, here it is…

GANG BANGIN IS DEAD!

That's right—just like the game, Gang Bangin is over with too. In today's time, no matter what set you claim, Gang Bangin is not even a reckoning dilemma anymore. Don't get it twisted though, once upon a time, it did use to be a major problem in the United States. Dating all the way back to more than two hundred years ago. But if you study the history of gangs in America, you will discover the glimpsing truth that Gang Bangin was only a problem when it intertwined with several issues, ranging from social, political to economic concern.

Initially, Gang Bangin became a social concern when gangs were being formed to protect black people who were facing violent attacks from white gangs (who originated gangs, BTW). This led to the widespread of black gangs in New York, which included the Huns, Devil Hunters, and The Farmers. There was so much square-business fighting going down between the white and black gangs that it was considered to be a threat to National Security.

In the 1960s, one of the major gang events that was witnessed during this time was the formation of the 18th Street Gang, which became a major rival with the MS-13. In 1965, several gang sets came together to form an alliance that was aimed at resisting the Watts Rebellion.

After a successful rebellion, gang members diverted their efforts and started joining political parties with aggressive intentions to start movements.

For instance, Bunchy Carter, a former OG, rose to become head of the Black Panther Party in Los Angeles. Other OGs including Hakim Jamal, William Sampson, Robaire Nyjuky, and Ron Wilkins, just to name a few.

Likewise, there was a rivalry between police officers and gangs in the mid-60s with a fatal clash in August of 1965, where 34 people were left dead with over a thousand others wounded during the Watts Riots. This period also saw the formation of the Black Power Movement, which you know damn well led to political concern.

In the 1970's Stanley "Tookie" Williams at 16, and his 15-year-old homie Raymond Washington, started a set called the Baby Avenues in order to replace the Black Power Movement. The gang later came to be known as what we are all familiar with today: The Crips (which initially started as the acronym: Community Reform Inner-Party Service), with intentions to protect the community. Crips encountered resistance due to rivalry with other gangs, eventually leading to pistol play. This resulted in the merging of non-Crip gangs to form "The Bloods." By 1974, Bloods and Crips were active in several regions throughout LA covering an area of up to 30 square miles. The shooting of Raymond in August 1979 crunked up pistol play to a whole different level.

In the 1980s and 90s, gangs in America were introduced to Crack Cocaine—devastating not only the South Central region with Bloods and Crips but damn near every other region of the United States that was involved in selling and coppin the drug. As a result, high crime rates spread throughout all parts of the country, resulting in what is known as Mass Incarceration. In the 1990s, gang activity and police brutality against black people increased, with the L.A riots being televised all over the country.

Ironically, gang activity (as a whole) didn't receive Presidential condemnation from Bill Clinton until the murder of three-year-old Stephanie Kuhen.

Question! Is it not a coincidence that gang activity in America was not (and still is not) a major concern until it affects this country's social, political, or economic affairs?

Almost every well-known gang in America started as a political gang, and if you read the history of GDs and the Vicelords, you'll pretty much discover the same thing.

Furthermore, ask yourself if gang activity is a problem or a national concern today? HELL NO! Wait a minute—how can that be when gang activity attributes to a number of other factors, including but not limited to increased drug trafficking, easy access to guns, poverty, and unemployment among the black youth? How can that be when there are bodies dropping like flies in the city of Chicago alone (contributing to 661 gang-related deaths in the year 2017)? Why? Because what is known as gang activity today does not (directly or indirectly) affect "The Beast" in the least.

IT ONLY CONTRIBUTES TO IT! As long as we have our attention and hatred focused on each other, then we are not a threat to anyone (or anything) but ourselves.

WHICH REMINDS ME!

The Willie Lynch Syndrome. This syndrome is derived from a speech given by Willie Lynch (a British slave owner) on the bank of the James River in the Colony of Virginia in 1712.

December 25, 1712: Gentlemen,

> I greet you here on the bank of the James River in the year of our Lord, one thousand seven hundred and twelve.

First, I shall thank you, the Gentlemen of the Colony of Virginia, for bringing me here. I am here to help you solve some of your problems with slaves. Your invitation reached me on my modest plantation in the West Indies, where I have experimented with some of the newest and still the oldest methods for the control of slaves.

Ancient Rome would envy us if my program is implemented. As our boat sailed south on the James River, named for our illustrious King James, whose Bible we cherish, I saw enough to know that your problem is not unique.
While Rome used cords of wood as crosses for standing human bodies along the old highways in great numbers, you are here using the tree and the rope on occasion.
I caught the whiff of a dead slave hanging from a tree a couple of miles back. You are not only losing valuable stock by hangings, you are having uprisings, slaves are running away, your crops are sometimes left in the fields too long for maximum profit, you suffer occasional fires, your animals are killed, gentlemen.... You know what your problems are; I do not need to elaborate. I am not here to enumerate your problems; I am here to introduce to you to a method of solving them.
In my bag here, I have a fool-proof method for controlling your Black slaves.

I guarantee every one of you that if installed correctly, it will control the slaves for at least 300 years. My method is simple, any member of your family or any overseer can use it.

I have outlined a number of differences among the slaves, and I take these differences and make them bigger. I use fear, distrust, and envy for control purposes.

These methods have worked on my modest plantation in the West Indies, and it will work throughout the South. Take this simple little list of differences and think about them. On the top of my list "Age," but it is there because it only starts with an "A"; the second is "Color" or shade; there is intelligence, size, sex, size of plantations, attitude of owners, whether the slaves living in the valley, on a hill, East, West, North, South, have fine or coarse hair, or is tall or short.

Now that you have a list of differences, I shall give you an outline of action—but before that, I shall assure you that distrust is stronger than trust, and envy is stronger than adulation, respect or admiration.

The Black Slave, after receiving this indoctrination, shall carry on and will become self-refueling and self- generating for hundreds of years, maybe thousands.

Don't forget, you must pitch the old Black vs. the young Black male and the young Black male against the old Black male. You must use the dark skin slaves vs. the light skin slaves, and the light skin slaves vs. the dark skin slaves. You must use the female vs. the male, and the male vs. the female.

You must also have your servants and overseers distrust all Blacks, but it is necessary that your slaves trust and depend on us. They must love, respect and trust only us.

Gentlemen, these kits are your keys to control, use them. Have your wives and children use them. Never miss the opportunity. My plan is guaranteed, and the good thing about this plan is that if used intensely for one year, the slaves themselves will remain perpetually distrustful of each other.

Thank you, gentlemen.

WHO IS THE OPPOSITION?

Slavery has posttraumatic mental illnesses that severely affects us (black people) even today. So if you are SET-Trippin with someone based on what hood (or color flag) they rep. Better yet, if you are Gang Bangin within this prison industrial complex (The institutional descendant of slave plantations, that feeds off black pain and black loss) ask yourself the following questions:

1) Am I experiencing the Willie Lynch Syndrome?
2) Who is the opposition? Is it someone who's in the same predicament as myself?

3) What was the purpose of (Name of your gang) when it started?
4) What is the purpose of (Name of your gang) now?
5) Where am I headed with this?
6) Am I going to pass this down to my children?
7) Do I REALLY want to go home?
8) Then why am I jeopardizing my opportunity of making parole by risking my status, thus making it even that much harder to do so?
9) What race of people started gangs in America? What race showed me how to be Gangsta, have evil thoughts, and nefarious intentions? What race showed me how to beat my children, make them scared shitless of me, and even going to the extent of making them go get their own switch from a tree? What race showed me what HATE really means?
10) Hold up! I thought Rick said that racism was played out?

Note from the author: Racism is dead, Homie! The powers at be no longer have to focus on hating us since we do such a great job at hating ourselves.

Keynote: It was predetermined that we would hate and fight each other for at least 300 to a thousand years.

```
   1712
+   300
────────
   2012
```

So since we are eight years past the 300-year mark (and we are still fighting and killing each other) are we going to go ahead and shoot for a cool thousand?

Note from author: In no way am I implying or making a supposition that you should practice hate towards white people. My sole premise for writing this chapter was to paint a picture of how fucking stupid we look.

That's why I started it with an example with Suga Bear. Everything that we rep: Pimp-N, Gang Bangin, Thug-Life, Jack Game, Murder Game, Trapp-N, etc...it's all CLOWN SHIT!!!

And the ones who are dying and catching double- and triple-digit sentences for staying dedicated soldiers have no idea of where THE GAME originated. However, to practice hate is to continue reproducing the bullshit we were taught. Love is a higher and much greater force that does not relinquish to enmity. So practice love instead! But before you can love anyone else, the main person who you are going to have to learn how to love is YOURSELF.

MESSAGE TO THE REAL NIGGA

I promise you on everything that I genuinely love, I'm going to win before and after I touch down. I attest to that with determined and squinted eyes. But guess what? I want you to win too. I want you to develop some type of purpose that will alter your perception of life (and where you want to be) and start working towards it. But you have to want it though! You have to want to give up the watered-down version of what so many convicts consider to be REAL. So, what I'm about to do right now is, call out all the so-called REAL NIGGAS. I challenge you right here today to make a real difference. Show that 20-something-year-old-youngsta who just stepped through the door that wasting time is equivalent to wasting money. Show them that the crimes we committed, the street-life we chased, and the lives that were taken is all an artificial lifestyle (if it's not beneficial, it's artificial).

If you took a life, then here's your opportunity to save one. If you are on this list, then that means I consider you to have "INFLUENCE," which is the number one implementation needed in order to make a difference. If you are on this list, then I also know that you have "RESPECT." Put it like this—I know that your name is ringing within the system. Therefore, I also know that your word is valued upon and considered in its highest regard. (If, however, you are in another state other than Texas and you know that your word holds weight and that you possess the above qualifications, then I'm talking to you too). Use that SUPREME POWER to not only make a difference but give the unenlightened...THE REAL GAME!

1) Julian "FATZ" Burt
2) Baby Ca$h
3) Tarzan
4) South Park Mexican (Carlos Coy)
5) Sir Brandon
6) Ra Ra (Randy Arroyo)
7) Prince (Jordan Unit)
8) Squirrel (Jordan Unit)
9) Lil Jap (Jordan Unit)
10) Chaos (Sylvester Spraggins
11) M.K.
12) Cedrick Rose
13) Bat Man
14) Kevin McFail (Dollar Bill
15) Michael Ray
16) Taco
17) Pimp Black
18) Big D. (Derick)
19) Travis Wilson (Big Kool-Aid)

Considering that was a (let's say) INTENSE subject I just expounded on, I guess I'll drop a brain teaser on you so we can lower the tension levels a little bit. It's titled:

The Light Switch

The warden of a small minimum-security prison believes that everyone deserves a second chance. He rounds up the 20 prisoners in his prison and offers to release them if they can solve his puzzle. Each of the 20 prisoners will be placed alone in solitary confinement. The warden will then draw a name at random and bring the prisoner to an empty building. Inside the building is a light switch that does nothing. The prisoner can flip the switch up or down if they like, after which they'll be escorted back to their cell.

Sometime later, the warden will bring another prisoner at random to the empty building with the light switch.

Once again, the prisoner can flip the switch up or down if they like, after which they'll be escorted back to their cell. Note that the same prisoner might be selected multiple times before some prisoners are selected at all.

This will continue until one of the prisoners tells the warden that all 20 of them have been to the empty building with the light switch at least once. If the prisoner is right, they will all be released. If the prisoner is wrong, the group loses their chance for immediate release. "Oh, one more thing, the light switch is currently in the DOWN position," the warden tells the prisoners.

The prisoners have one hour to come up with a plan to solve the puzzle. When the hour is up, they will be escorted to their solitary confinement, and there will be no further communication of any kind between them.

Can you figure out the answer? Note that this is NOT a trick question—the answer lies in some kind of coordinated switch-flipping strategy.

HINT: All the prisoners except for one have to follow some kind of plan while the remaining one (the counter) does something a little different that will allow him to keep a record of how many prisoners have flipped the switch. ANSWER ON NEXT PAGE.

ANSWER: First, the prisoners elect someone to be the Counter. When any prisoner besides the Counter enters the building, they will flip the switch to the up position if it is down AND if they have not previously flipped the switch to the up position. Otherwise, they do nothing. The Counter, on the other hand, never flips the switch to the up position. When the Counter enters the building, if the switch is in the up position, they will flip it down and add one to their "Prisoner Count." If the switch is already in the down position, they do nothing. This way, each of the prisoners, besides the Counter, will flip the switch up only once arid the Counter will flip the switch down once for each of the other 19 prisoners. Once the Counter has flipped the switch down 19 times, they'll know that every prisoner has been to the building with the light switch at least once.

Chapter 8

THE ONE THING

Now that you have mastered your environment and placed a chokehold on your habits, it's now time to focus on the one thing. People are starting to understand that you are a leader. One of the hardest things about being a leader, whether you're the manager at McDonald's, the CEO of a business, or even a speaker for a gang, is that you have to make decisions that make a lot of people unhappy. That's why they say that it's lonely at the top because an effective leader can tolerate the resentment from others.

But seeing how you've put your foot on the neck of the fear, or criticism by reaching a decision not to worry about what other people think, do or say, you can now draw your energy towards the one thing. Remember, the one thing is what you plan to do when you touch down.

Nevertheless, it's something that you have to put down right now, though. On the grounds that you know you cannot act where you are not, you cannot act where you have been, and you cannot act where you are going to be—you can only act where you are right now. How that works is, if you plan to be a sports announcer something similar to Steven A. Smith, then you should stay glued to Sports Center from sun up to sun down because it will broadcast valuable information that will benefit you towards your future job. Likewise, if you plan to hustle at the casinos in Vegas, then you should stay glued to the knock table the same amount of time because by the time you get out of here, you will have become an expert at knowing the perfect time and opportunity when to drop. Now, keep in mind that if you don't plan to be a sports announcer, or if Vegas doesn't even know what the hell a game of knock is, then my dude, you are wasting your time and energy.

When you are Pimp-N The Pen, there's no such thing as wasting time, passing time, or killing time. Pimp-N The Pen means that you are TAKING ADVANTAGE OF TIME! Luckily the pen is absolutely full of interesting things to do. Only lack of imagination or lack of energy stand in your way.

Otherwise, each of us could be established authors, artists, physical fitness trainers, film directors, business owners, entrepreneurs, poets, musicians, inventors, scholars, activists, etc. Because mostly everything I put down is usually about creating, I admit that sometimes I get too caught up on the creative process. I'll get so excited about a book idea or an art project or a fire ass poem that I'll forget that not everyone shares the passion to assist the creative process. It's important to remember that not everyone is a Wahida Clark, or a Mike Enemigo, or a Darius Clark Monroe, or a Nathan McCall. Some people just aren't creative like that. Better yet, maybe it's that they think they're not creative.

Everyone has a story. From my experience in the pen, I've heard story after story, and each time that particular convict told it, he became more creative in switching it up so the story could sound better the next time he told it.

Believe it or not, but he has the potential to write an urban novel. So don't consume urban novels, WRITE THEM! However, there is nothing wrong with supporting an author who is currently on lock. But don't read it merely for entertainment (getting caught up in a pipe dream of a dude moving a gazillion tons of work) or don't throw it in the back of your locker and only pull it out during lock-down. On the other hand, study it. Peep how he managed to capture your attention within the first 10 pages (which is the secret to any successful book).

Also, you can choose an urban novel that you know well. List the two or three main characters. Ask yourself if any of them seem to have a conflict between two values or desires in the story? If so, locate the scenes in which the character demonstrates each one.

Then find and study the scene in which he chooses between the two values. How does the author indicate his inner chaos? You with me? Ok, now list five values that you believe in. Can you imagine a situation in which any of them might come in conflict with another? Which would you choose? There you go—there's a story that you might want to put down.

I wrote Threat To The World (which was my first book) a couple of years ago at the Allred Unit. I wrote it as a symbolical indication to myself or any other typical representative of the game. I was inspired to write it because too many people (myself included) have spent the majority of our lives dedicated to a game that has no benefits and no guarantees except a dead-end destination. In the conclusion of Threat To The World, my main character (Threat) realizes that he was dreaming and, as a result, is awakened to a countless number of psychological issues. Which in essence is the significance of the mental status that

so many of us in the game have but unfortunately don't realize. All of us, at some point, have been trapped inside of a phantasmic fantasy with the symptoms of antisocial by virtue of insanity characteristics.

Einstein's definition of insanity is doing the same thing over and over while expecting different results each time.

I was able to write Threat To The World like nothing because it is the direct reflection of my belief system. Once I became a better writer, I was able to write other fiction novels that were the total opposite of my tenet principles.

Which was beneficial because not only did it enhance my writing skills, but while writing it, I was completely free of any prison institutionalized thoughts.

Writing is my one thing because when I touch down, I'm going to write and direct stage plays. When I become large and successful, I plan to come back into the prisons (as a volunteer this time) so I can share my success story in hopes of inspiring other convicts that they too can leave prison as a winner. I'm going to show by example that a setback is not permanent failure. It only means that your plans weren't solid. That means to build another plan.

Start all over again. But make sure it's positive, productive, and realistic next time. Going positive, you are guaranteed to come out on top. A certified winner!

Although every winner has a past. When society thinks of formerly incarcerated people, they more than likely focus on our previous actions instead of our humanity. The term "Criminal," which tends to be tossed at us as an insult, brings to mind images of terrifying thugs unworthy of respect or compassion. But with about 2.3 million people currently on lock, the United States has the world's largest prison population. And despite the fact that black people and Hispanics make up only one-quarter of the general US population, combined, we comprise 58% of the prison population.

But what if society thought of us not as pariahs, but as full human beings with the capacity to use our prison experience to change the world? Some formerly incarcerated convicts have done just that, and by focusing on the one thing, they managed to defy the odds they would normally face in a society where it's difficult to destroy the stereotypes aimed at an ex-convict. Using tools like physical fitness, authorship, education, film-making, activism, etc.

These world changers have shifted the culture and system of incarceration in the U.S. Their work is a reminder that prison time and criminal convictions are not the sum total of a convicted felon. As Pac once said, "They messed up when they gave me time to think."

The following people Pimped The Pen as well by taking advantage of their time. They remind me of sailors, because back in the gap when sailors used to get lost in a storm, they'd always look for the north star for guidance. They could use that star to help them get their bearings because it never moved in the sky. You have to use the one thing the same way.

Whenever you face obstacles or hurdles in life, look to the one thing. As long as you've frozen it in your mind and it never moves, you'll know which direction to go in. As long as you never lose sight of it, you'll never lose sight of success either.

MALCOLM X

In the 1950s, Malcolm X's prison education became his one thing as it was a dramatic example of how a convict can have the ability to turn "INCARCERATION" into a transformative experience. With no available means of organizing his quest for knowledge, he proceeded to read a dictionary, copying each word in his own hand.

Once he had started re-educating himself, there was no limit to his search for fact and inspiration. Through Norfolk's prison library, Malcolm devoured the writings of influential scholars such as W.E.B. DuBois, Carter G. Woodson, and J.A. Rogers. He studied the history of the transatlantic slave trade, the impact of the "Peculiar Institution" of chattel slavery in the United States, and African-American revolts. He learned with satisfaction about Nat Turner's 1831 uprising in Virginia, which to him, provided a clear example of black resistance.

Nor did Malcolm restrict his studies solely to Black History. He plowed through Herodotus, Kant, Nietzsche, and other historians and philosophers of Western civilization. He was impressed by Mahatma Gandhi's accounts of the struggle to drive the British out of India—he was shocked by the history of China's opium wars, and the European and American Suppression of the 1901 Boxer Rebellion.

The following narrative comes from his autobiography, The Autobiography Of Malcolm X (1965) which he wrote with Alex Haley:

> Many who today hear me somewhere in person, or on television, or those who read something I've said, will think I went to school far beyond the eighth grade. This impression is due entirely to my prison studies.

It had really begun back in the Charlestown Prison when Bimbi first made me feel envy of his stock of knowledge. Bimbi had always taken charge of any conversations he was in,

and I had tried to emulate him. But every book I picked up had few sentences which didn't contain anywhere from one to nearly all of the words that might as well have been in Chinese. When I just skipped those words, of course, I really ended up with little idea of what the book said. So I had come to the Norfolk Prison Colony still going through only book-reading motions. Pretty soon, I would have quit even these motions, unless I had received the motivation that I did.

I saw that the best thing I could do was get hold of a dictionary - to study, to learn some words. I was lucky enough to reason also that I should try to improve my penmanship. It was sad. I couldn't even write in a straight line. It was both ideas together that moved me to request a dictionary along with some tablets and pencils from the Norfolk Prison Colony school.

I spent two days just riffling uncertainly through the dictionary's pages. I'd never realized so many words existed! I didn't know which words I needed to learn. Finally, just to start some kind of action, I began copying.

In my slow, painstaking, ragged handwriting, I copied into my tablet everything printed on that first page, down to the punctuation marks.

I believe it took me a day. Then, aloud, I read back, to myself, everything I'd written on the tablet. Over and over, aloud, to myself, I read my own handwriting.

I woke up the next morning, thinking about those words— immensely proud to realize that not only had I written so much at one time, but I'd written words that I never knew were in the world. Moreover, with a little effort, I also could remember what many of these words meant. I reviewed the words whose meanings I didn't remember. Funny thing, from the dictionary first page right now, that "aardvark" springs to my mind. The dictionary had a picture of it, a long-tailed, long-eared, burrowing African mammal, which lives off termites caught by sticking out its tongue as an anteater, does for ants.

I was so fascinated that I went on—I copied the dictionary's next page. And the same experience came when I studied that. With every succeeding page, I also learned of people and places and events from history. Actually, the dictionary is like a miniature encyclopedia. Finally, the dictionary's A section had filled a whole tablet and I went on into the B's. That was the way I started copying what eventually became the entire dictionary. It went a lot faster after so much practice helped me to pick up handwriting speed. Between what I wrote in my tablet and writing letters, during the rest of my time in prison, I would guess I wrote a million words.

I suppose it was inevitable that as my word-base broadened, I could, for the first, time pick up a book and read and now begin to understand what the book was saying. Anyone who has read a great deal can imagine the new world that opened. Let me tell you something: from then until I left that prison, in every free moment I had, if I was not reading in the library, I was reading on my bunk. You couldn't have gotten me out of books with a wedge. Between Mr. Muhammad's teachings, my correspondence, my visitors... and my reading of books, months passed without my even thinking about being imprisoned. In fact, up to then, I never had been so truly free in my life.

The Norfolk Prison Colony's library was in the school building. A variety of classes was taught there by instructors who came from such places as Harvard and Boston universities. The weekly debates between inmate teams were also held in the school building. You would be astonished to know how worked up convict debaters and audiences would get over subjects like "Should Babies Be Fed Milk?"

Available on the prison library's shelves were books on just about every general subject. Much of the big private collection that Parkhurst had willed to the prison was still in crates and boxes in the back of the library—thousands of old books.

Some of them looked ancient: covers faded, old-time parchment-looking binding. Parkhurst. . . seemed to have been principally interested in history and religion. He had the money and the special interest to have a lot of books that you wouldn't have in a general circulation. Any college library would have been lucky to get that collection.

As you can imagine, especially in a prison where there was a heavy emphasis on rehabilitation, an inmate was smiled upon if he demonstrated an unusually intense interest in books. There was a sizable number of well-read inmates, especially the popular debaters. Some were said by many to be practically walking encyclopedias. They were almost celebrities. No university would ask any student to devour literature as I did when this new world opened to me, of being able to read and UNDERSTAND.

I read more in my room than in the library itself. An inmate who was known to read a lot could check out more than the permitted maximum number of books. I preferred reading in the total isolation of my own room.

When I had progressed to really serious reading, every night at about ten P.M., I would be outraged with the "lights out." It always seemed to catch me right in the middle of something engrossing.

Fortunately, right outside my door was a corridor light that cast a glow into my room. The glow was enough to read by, once my eyes adjusted to it. So when "lights out" came, I would sit on the floor where I could continue reading in that glow.

At one-hour intervals at night, guards paced past every room. Each time I heard the approaching footsteps, I jumped into bed and feigned sleep. And as soon as the guard passed, I got back out of bed onto the floor area of that light-glow, where I would read for another fifty-eight minute until the guard approached again.

That went on until three or four every morning. Three or four hours of sleep a night was enough for me. Often in the years in the streets, I had slept less than that.

I have often reflected upon the new vistas that reading opened to me. I knew right there in prison that reading had changed forever the course of my life. As I see it today, the ability to read awoke inside me some long dormant craving to be mentally alive. I certainly wasn't seeking any degree, the way a college confers a status symbol upon its students. My homemade education gave me, with every additional book that I read, a little bit more sensitivity to the deafness, dumbness, and blindness that was afflicting the black race in America.

Not long ago, an English writer telephoned me from London, asking questions. One was, "What's your alma mater?" I told him, "Books." You will never catch me with a free fifteen minutes in which I'm not studying something I feel might be able to help the black man.

Every time I catch a plane, I have with me a book that I want to read and that's a lot of books these days. If I weren't out here every day battling the white man, I could spend the rest of my life reading, just satisfying my curiosity—because you can hardly mention anything I'm not curious about. I don't think anybody ever got more out of going to prison than I did.

In fact, prison enabled me to study far more intensively than I would have if my life had gone differently, and I had attended some college. I imagine that one of the biggest troubles with colleges is there are too many distractions, too much panty-raiding, fraternities, and boola-boola and all of that. Where else but in a prison could I have attacked my ignorance by being able to study intensely sometimes as much as fifteen hours a day?

Question:

Malcolm X has been quoted as saying that 5-to-10 years of prison time was the best thing for a black man to experience. Why do you think Malcolm prescribed prison to the black man?

Prior to going to prison, Malcolm's formal education did not exceed beyond the eighth grade. At the same time, he was street-savvy and considered to be a Jack-of-all-Trades. However, when he re-educated himself, he discovered a broad and new understanding of the world. Do you think many of us (Gangstas, Pimps, Dope Sellers, and Street Thugs) are just like Malcolm (SMART) but haven't really applied ourselves to re-educating our understanding of the world?

What's the first word that comes to your mind when you think of Malcolm?

_____

So is it safe to say that knowledge really is power?

What I suggest:

Get plenty of it (KNOWLEDGE) while you have the time and perfect opportunity. Also ask someone on your wing who you know has the book Knowledge of Self.

Once you get it, scroll all the way down to the last sentence on page 184 and continue with the same sentence on page 185.

WAHIDA CLARK

From inmate to four-time New York Times best-selling author, Wahida Clark, has become one of the most sought after urban lit authors of this generation, and is one of only four urban lit authors to appear on the New York Times bestseller list. She is the only urban lit author on the list to have also served time.

Wahida Clark has what you would call an amazing story. Tenacity, vison, and sheer determination are what helped her rise to become the successful author and businesswoman she is today.

She began writing her first novel while serving a nine- year bid, including nine months in solitary confinement, at the Lexington Prison Camp in Lexington, KY. While behind bars, she inked publishing deals with two major publishing houses, wrote and released seven novels, including one New York Times bestseller, and laid the groundwork for her own publishing company,

Wahida Clark Presents, with the help of media queen, mentor, and prison mate MARTHA STEWART.

This is a full interview where she tells JET magazine about the nine years she spent in jail, her proactive pursuit in writing novels, and the start of her own publishing company.

JET: How did you begin writing novels?

Clark: I started writing while I was incarcerated. I was sentenced to nine years in federal prison, and I had to do something to take care of myself while in prison. I had two teenage daughters, my husband was incarcerated, and I needed to set up a foundation for us to have when I got home.

Jet: Why did you go to prison?

Clark: I went to prison for mail fraud, wire fraud, and money laundering.

JET: What were you doing before you went to prison?

Clark: I was an entrepreneur. I had a print shop, I had marketing telecommunication products, I was also into sales. I always had my own business.

JET: Did you always want to be a writer?

Clark: Not at all. I hadn't written before in my life. I had No clue. I didn't even know I could write.

JET: Why did you become an author?

Clark: One day, I, called home, and I said, "guys send me some money," and they said, "We'll see what we can do." They said, "Wahida they are foreclosing your house, you're losing everything, all your businesses are shutting down— you're not here to run it. We're going to shut everything down and move back to up to Jersey." My family was living in Georgia at the time. I got off the phone and started praying and thinking, "what can I do?"

I was working in the library at the time, and one morning I was looking through a magazine and saw an article about Shannon Holmes. It said that he wrote a book while he was in prison, the book was called B-More Careful. So I'm sitting there, staring at the bookshelves, and I start to visualize my name on the spines of the books: Wahida Clark, Wahida Clark. And I had my light bulb moment. I said I'm going to write me a book.

JET: How did you get your first publishing deal?

Clark: I have a habit of reading the acknowledgments in books, and I would always see Carl Weber's name. So after I finished reading one of his books, I said I'm going to write this brother and see what happens.

Right after I closed his book, I wrote him a letter saying: Hey Carl, I'm a big fan of yours. Right now, I'm locked up, but I just finished writing my first book, I don't even have a title yet, but I'm investigating print-on-demand companies, do you have any suggestions? I mailed the letter. I actually didn't expect him to write back, but he did. He said he had just started his own publishing company and for me to send him my manuscript. The first person I sent a manuscript to, I got a publishing deal.

Jet: What's your writing process?

Clark: I just write. I get a pen and paper and start writing. I handwrite everything, and it takes anywhere from three-to-five months. Once I start writing, the characters really take on a life of their own.

JET: How were you able to come out of prison successful? How did you stay mentally strong?

Clark: My husband gave me words to live by, he said "Don't waste time; stay busy."

JET: Tell me about your breakthrough in the novel world.

Clark: When I left the prison in 2007, I already had seven books published, I had made the Essence Magazine bestsellers list, USA Today bestsellers list and the New York Times bestsellers list. I had two publishing deals with major companies, I had an agent, and I already had my business plan for my publishing company.

JET: What does it take to become a New York Times bestseller?

Clark: Building a fan base, connecting with your readers, and hustling. Gone are the days where you can write a book and sit back and think it's going to sell itself. You have to be in hustle mode, especially in our genre, you have to be creative. For writers, creativity is the product.

In order to move that product, you have to hustle. I had to brand myself, brand my product, and brand my book.

JET: What inspires you?

Clark: The characters motivate me to tell their story to get their words on paper.

JET: How many more books for the "Thug Series" do you plan to write?

Clark: You know there are five books in the series: Thugs and the Women Who Love Them, Every Thug Needs a Lady, Thug Matrimony, Thug Lovin', Justify My Thug. Part six of the thug series is coming out soon. I have a lot of readers for the thug series. My character now has books out, that's how much my readers like the characters. Tasha Macklin's book just came out titled Baller Dreams. Trae's book is coming out in a couple of weeks titled Flippin, the Hustle. My readers love the characters, they support them. My characters have twitter pages and Facebook fan pages.

JET: What are your future plans?

Clark: Actually, I'm just getting started. I'm working on a play, people are looking over the books for movies. I have my own publishing company with fifteen authors and 25 books in stores throughout the country...I'm just getting started.

Question:

In the book Think and Grow Rich, Napoleon Hill said "If you do not see great riches in your imagination, you will never see them in your bank balance." If you notice in this interview, Wahida Clark said that she visualized her name on the spines of the books in the library where she worked: Wahida Clark, Wahida Clark...VISUALIZATION is the number one rule to the Law of Attraction. With that being said, what do you see yourself accomplishing by the time the doors open up to you?

Fill in the blank

Before I get out of here, I see myself accomplishing:

1)

2)

3)

4)

MIKE ENEMIGO

Beginning 20 years ago, the man behind the self-styled pen name, Mike Enemigo, has been serving Life Without The Possibility of Parole. He's been part of the 300% increase in state spending on corrections, directly related to the expanding number of people incarcerated in the United States.

Considering the effect LWOP can have on a convict is important, especially when you have someone like Mike who is (rare as it is) actually rehabilitating himself and working towards pro-social goals in the process. Mike's One Thing became his publishing project—The Cell Block, which is more than enough confirmation that success is still possible while pulling even a life sentence. Mike has done more than waste of time. In his own words, he is becoming the figure of a new role model, which is most definitely emerging.

So...Welcome to The Cell Block headquarters: A 9' X 5' cell.

The interview is given by Anthony Tinsman.

Anthony Tinsman: In your book The Enemy Of The State, you were committed to music, smuggling in a recorder, and smuggling out tapes from a cell. The pieces just didn't come together. Unlike your publishing company, The Cell Block, which has had some success. Your attempts at a music career had influenced. Who were some influences that pushed you towards publishing? I mean, your Aunt Fran sent urban literature to help with research, but did you meet any authors inside. What's that story?

Enemigo: I'd have to say that my biggest influence to begin writing and publishing books was my failure to be able to get my music done and released the way I wanted from my cell. I didn't have anyone to teach me to do all this. I had to teach myself by falling and learning, essentially, what not to do.

Each time I'd bust a move that didn't work out the way I'd hoped, I'd reflect on what I could adjust to ensure that it never happened again. Slowly but surely, I started to see that books were where it's going to be at for me. Given my situation, I relied on many people and the very rare windows of opportunity in prison, in order to accomplish my goals [with music], but with books, I was able to see the "urban" book game the same way as the "rap" game, and producing a book was the same as producing a CD, just different media: but, of course, one I have a much stronger possibility to make a strong impact in. So I've been on it ever since, and as you mentioned, now I'm grabbing some form of success.

That was my biggest influence - survival. Once I decided it was books I needed to be doing, I asked my mom to send me English grammar for Dummies, and I began stepping my grammar game up. I needed to see what the standard was like for urban books, as I hadn't read many at the time, so I asked my pops to buy me a few. He don't fuck with the computer, so he outsourced that to my Aunt Fran. The only books I knew of were some published by RJ Publications because I saw their ad in my XXL mag. So I ordered eight. At this time, where I was deciding books were going to be my answer, someone was selling 50 Cent's From Pieces to Weight on the tier. I snatched it up, read it, and saw how bad the writing was -and this was a 50 Cent book! That gave me confidence.
Again, at this time, my cell-mate had given me a black men's magazine to flip through before he threw it out, and when I did, I saw a Seth Ferranti article/interview from his book Prison Stories.

Since he was actually doing what I wanted to do, I bought it, then *Street Legends* 1 & 2. Seth inspired me. It made what I was thinking that much more realistic. I think maybe the biggest thing I learned from Seth is that the difference between him and many others [prisoners with a dream], is that he actually took the steps to DO it. Here I was, across the country, in my prison cell, and I had a book in my hands that he created in his prison cell. This might not seem like much to someone reading this interview, but it was a very valuable and powerful lesson.

AT: Organization is everything. Dan Poynter said that. He was the "ombudsman" of independent publishing. He also said, "Most people have what it takes. The hard part is getting organized." Describe your office, and how does your schedule mesh with the penitentiary?

Enemigo: Organization is definitely a must. Luckily for me, I'm OCD. Once I zero in on something, I can't stop thinking about it until it's done. So I use the 'disorder' to my advantage. Where many people may procrastinate and be disorganized, I can't do that. When I'm not working on my project, odds are I'm thinking about at least some aspect of it: reorganizing, adjusting, improving, etc.

My office? [It's] my prison cell, which is also TCB headquarters. I change my office and the headquarters location when I'm moved to a new prison cell. Others can determine where my office is located, but they cannot determine whether or not I have an office. I keep things organized and uncluttered. It helps me breathe. I sit on my rack [bunk] with my typewriter on my lap most of the day, working on something: a project, a letter to a family member, friends, colleagues, or fans, whatever.

Sometimes, when I really get into my zone and don't want to be interrupted, I may have stacks of paper and my Macmillan dictionary around me, and it may look messy, but I know exactly what's what. It is only "messy" because I'm in my zone and don't want to take time to put things back in their place.

I don't let the penitentiary dictate what I do and don't do. Sure, there are some things I cannot change. I treat it/them like a pothole in the road. I just go around it. I ignore most things about the penitentiary. I do not care about the penitentiary.

AT: Ten books published since January 2014. That's a lot of work; so, too, is maintaining a network of authors in state prisons, like Folsom, Chino, Tehachapi, and others.
What are some things you would do differently if you had known what you know now?

Enemigo: Ten books from my prison cell is absolutely a lot of work. Maintaining my network of people, many of whom are prisoners all over the country, is very exhausting. Had I known when I started what I know now, what I would have done different is, I'd have focused more on building "Mike Enemigo" rather than "TCB." I would have concentrated my forces more than I did. But it's good. I can sign a deal with a major urban publisher right now and give them 20 books for their catalog.
That's a cake.

AT: What did the book release party look like for your newest title? My celebrations have gotten tame as I get older. They used to boil over for days of smoking and cheap wine. You got any rituals?

Enemigo: I don't have release parties. Ten books in. Not one party.

When I'm done with a book, I send it out, unclutter everything in my cell that accumulated as a result of the project, then get organized and ready for the next one.

That's what I do. A few months later, once I finally receive a retail-ready copy of the book, I get some sort of satisfaction at seeing and holding it "fresh," how most people will see it for the first time, without all the ugliness and hard work that goes into it. That is my reward, and it lasts about a day. Maybe two. A few months later, I get tired of looking at it on my shelf, and I give it away. My drug is replacing it with a new one, and I'm addicted to that. I fiend for it.

AT: What are your favorite books, authors, and entertainers? What are you reading now?

Enemingo: I haven't had a chance to read many books lately. I'm too busy creating books for others to read. Entertainers? TV: TMZ, Shark Tank, and Big Brother. Music: Drake and Nipsey Hussle.

AT: You're doing life. Most authors dream of celebrity and wealth, but few get there. Why do you write? What are you getting out of it personally?

And why have you selected the "prison/street" market for most of your writing and authors?

Enemigo: Like many authors, I dream of wealth. Unlike many authors, I will get it. When I write, I write because I have something to say or an idea I think needs to be heard. I don't necessarily have a passion for the act of writing. I don't even like it much. But I enjoy saying what I have to say, expressing my thoughts and opinions, and writing is not only the way I'm able to do that best, but it's also the best way I have available to do it. If you notice, the books I write are how-to books, or my personal story - true shit. It's all something I feel I need to say so people can know my story, or learn something I want them to be enlightened upon.

I've selected the prisoner/street genre because, again, I come from hip-hop, and this is the stuff my authors and I are familiar with. We write what we know. Though I respect it because there are tons of dollars in it, I don't know trolls, zombies, vampires, and magical swords.

AT: You've written about the prison environment. About predators watching for "weakness" which can simply be not smashing someone if they call you a "bitch," that means you are a sex toy. A "bitch." But these automatic responses don't rely on thinking. Publishing does. Seth Ferranti, the founder of Gorilla Convict Publishing, summed it up when he said, "I'm not a criminal, I'm a businessman." Of course, he got into lower security prisons and got older before he said that shit. What events have changed your perspective? Made this possible?

Enemigo: I feel like Seth: I'm not a criminal, at least not anymore. I'm a businessman, I would like nothing more than to be free, running my business, whatever business, legally, and with all the opportunities and resources the freedom affords you. But that's not my reality. Reality is, I'm in prison, and prison has a culture that was established long before I got here, and I suspect it will be the same long after I'm gone. So whether I like it or not, I have to survive it. You can't play in the NFL according to the rules of the NBA. It's not going to work. Not only will you be unsuccessful, you will get hurt. This is something people out there fail to realize when some of us do what we do in here. But in the end, though I'd like to be understood, my ability to survive is more important to me than your ability to understand me.

AT: What's your take on prison reform? What laws would have to change to benefit you? And how would you determine your own legibility for relief?

Enemigo: I don't just have Life, I have Life Without Possibly of Parole, so much of the prison "reform" that takes place does not apply to me. So, I don't pay attention to it. I focus on reforming my personal prison experience and achieving all I can and living the best I can despite my reality. I have, however, recently heard something about people who were under the age of 23, who got sentenced to LWOP, being given an opportunity to possibly parole after 15-20 years. Something like that. That would apply to me. I was 19 at the time the crime I'm in prison for was committed, and thus far, I've been down since 1999.

Still waiting to hear more on that. My primary plan is to stack my money, get my case back in the forefront and hire an effective lawyer to go out and locate the witnesses I need that my original attorney failed to do and get a new trial. Money is the differentiator. If a law like the under 23 one I mentioned gets passed, maybe I'll invest my money in an attorney arguing my situation from that perspective. I have a few ideas, but they all require money.

Now, am I eligible to make it out there in the freeworld? Absolutely. I can honestly say I'm ready now. I've grown out of glorifying anything related to the prison lifestyle. I have no desire to do crime. I'm not looking for any problems, and I have the ability, especially with today's tech and opportunities, to make a ton of fuckin money, legally, even right from my own home, and that's enough for me. I don't need all the other shit. Just a cool spot where I can chill and do my thing over the internet, a decent stack of money and necessities, a bad bitch, and I'm good. Everything else is extra.

AT: What's your next project? Can we get a sneak peek?

Enemigo: I've got 10 books on my shelf, right now, ready to come out. Next will probably be Guru's book, *Underworld Zilla*. Underworld Zilla is a clique out of Sacramento, mostly Oak Park, that started as an answer to the cats from the Bay that were moving to the area trying to take over dope spots. Guru's book is not about the history of UZ, but it's connected to the movement.

Mark Sanders, aka MS, aka Manslaughta, aka Oak Park Mark, who is the co-founder of the Oak Park Bloods and is a Sac street legend, did the forward for the book. Guru's next book *Playboys* - Playboys is a term used by Riders to describe their lifestyle - will probably come out next. It's a fictional story but has true events and players mixed in -me, Bad Ass Snoop, etc. Then Guru has Sex, Money, Murder. I have two completed Ca$ciou$ Green books on the shelf - *For the Love of Blood Money* and *MOB $tars*. Probably release them soon. The first book I wrote, *Surviving Prison*, is ready. I just never put it out as of yet. Might drop that. I've got the *Hu$tlers Handbook for Prisoners* almost done. I've got some other things done and in the works, but everything I mentioned will probably drop before the end of 2016, as I'm setting up my pieces to go hard on marketing and promos this year.

AT: Any last words?

Enemigo: [Smiles] Stay tuned and be very afraid.

COSS MARTE

At an early age, Coss Marte felt like time was money, and he needed to spend all of it making more money. "A natural-born hustler," he called himself—and he became so successful as a dealer that he decided to devote himself to it full time. He was even hustling at The University of Albany, where just in his freshman year, he was expelled for (you guessed it) pushing work. But that didn't stop him—it only gave him the incentive to elevate his game to the next level.

At the age of 23, he was personally overseeing an empire that was pulling in $2 million a year in profit. "I felt like nobody could stop me." He says, now looking back. He was a small-time kingpin but living larger than life. He had everything that came with a baller's lifestyle: expensive cars, girls, gambling trips to Atlantic City, lavish Caribbean vacations—the whole nine.

But just like one of the fundamental laws of nature, what goes up must eventually come down. In 2009, Marte and his crew were hit hard by NYPD. Police raided his spot and found stacks of cash and more than a brick of cocaine.

After a bid at Rikers Island, Marte was sentenced to seven years upstate, where most of his time was spent at Greene Correctional Facility in Coxsackie, NY.

He said that prison altered his view of the world, that it really made him think about the stuff that he was doing before and how bad it was. The problems that he was causing, the effects on people's bodies— it really made him regret everything.

To pass his time, he started working out in his six- by-nine-foot cell, like most of us do when we hit the bricks. But Marte began developing his own form of exercise. He'd do pull-ups using a towel that was intertwined through the bars of his cell, and he'd wrap his mattress up like a backpack for squats.

He would put his feet on the toilet to do dips off his bed, and he also did planks from wall to wall.

Subsequently, he started running around the track on the yard. A first in prison, which caused a few laughs, but his unique workouts eventually drew in a crowd. Slowly but surely, it evolved into structured classes. He silenced everyone's laughs when he shed 70 pounds in just six months.

Marte was released after serving four years. By then, he'd perfected his workout regimen and completed his prison-offered college classes in psychology. When he returned to his old New York neighborhood, he began teaching his body-weight-only prison workout in the parks.

Today, the 30-year-old is considered a Fitness Guru with a dedicated following and a new gym called ConBody. He employed six instructors, five of whom also served time. His clientele ranges from neighborhood average Joes to millionaires like Dominic Suszanski, better known as the dude responsible for the selfie stick.

Marte invented his own HIIT body-weight routine with moves he conceived and named himself. He also custom-designed ConBody exercise playing cards that have specific workout instructions. He runs a 30-minute class that is all body-weight exercises that he created in prison. Also, he arranged it so that everyone has a "Prison Monkey" in class. He said that a prison monkey is your partner and will hold you accountable, pushing you. He said the most important value to working out with a partner is building camaraderie, a friendship that you most likely won't get in any other scenario.

Donald Ray Johnson is a motivational speaker and writer with a little over 4 years of experience in the publishing business. He is the leading author and co-founder of Southern Classic Publishing LLC, a Texas-based company whose mission is to make a bold statement from the south. He is the author of the urban classic BONA FIDE STREET THUG and many other novels that are to be released in the near future. In 2005 Donald was sentenced to prison, where he discovered his own ability to write street fiction. He is from Houston, Texas, and currently uses his time wisely, tutoring other incarcerated authors who are seeking to get into the business of publishing.

Shannon Holmes was born and raised in Bronx, New York. Holmes' entrance into the literary world was anything but ordinary. Armed with a GED and the desire to change his life, Holmes crafted his first novel and signed his first literary contract from prison, while serving a five-year sentence for various drug convictions. This was truly an amazing feat when you consider that Holmes had never even written a short story in his life. He truly made the best of a bad situation. He first achieved success with his first novel, B-more Careful, which sold half a million copies within one year. This may not sound like a lot of to the general public, but in the literary world, Holmes is platinum.

By producing such lofty sales numbers, Holmes was able to parlay the success of his first novel into a two-book, six- figure deal with publishing giant Simon & Schuster.

Avoiding the sophomore jinx, Holmes crafted the critically acclaimed Bad Girlz, which sold fifty thousand copies in its first week. His next novel, Never Go Home Again, received great reviews. With this, he achieved yet another milestone; he became the first author of the street genre to have his novel printed in hardcover.

Holmes then signed an even bigger deal publishing deal with St. Martin's Press, which was rumored to be in the high six figures for two novels. Shannon Holmes is a co-publisher of Triple Crown Publications.

Jeff Henderson served ten years for dealing and manufacturing cocaine as a youth. During his time in prison, he discovered he liked to cook and spent his days honing this talent. Released for good behavior, he worked as a chef in LA before moving to Las Vegas. He is currently working at Caesar's Palace, earning top recognition and rewards.

Darius Clark Monroe served three years of a five-year sentence at the Jim Ferguson Unit in Midway, Texas, for bank robbery. Last year, he completed Evolution of a Criminal, a feature-length autobiographical documentary executive produced by Spike Lee. The film, which the New Yorker called a "terrific movie," explores the various influences that pushed Monroe to rob a bank at age 16, like the fact that he grew up in a home with parents who struggled financially and whom he wanted to help. His decision would shape the rest of his life, and the film aims to help young people gain a sense of the ways their choices can affect the lives of many others. Monroe is currently using the film as a teaching tool, touring in high schools, juvenile detention centers, and prisons across the country. In a few weeks, 14 years after his release, Monroe will return to the Ferguson Unit to screen the film and discuss the ongoing ripple effects of mass incarceration.

Sean Pica entered prison as a 9th grade New Yorker with a 24-year sentence. He said he had little hope in himself or any sort of redemptive future. But, when he began reading children's books to fellow inmates and teaching them how to write letters to their loved ones, he witnessed how education created a flicker of joy amid the isolation.

Soon, he enrolled in an organization called Hudson Link, an education program in prisons (and Stand Together Foundation Catalyst), and took college classes. After he was released, he went on to earn 400 credits from Nyack College and two master's degrees from New York Theological Seminary and Hunter College. In 2007, Pica returned to lead Hudson Link as its Executive Director.

Today, Hudson Link's programs give education to thousands of men and women in prison, less than 4% of whom recidivate, compared to the rate of 67% nationwide. Pica's work saves New York State taxpayers over
$21 million per year and that number continues to increase.

Jayda Rasberry is a 28-year-old from Los Angeles who works as an organizer with Dignity And Power Now. In 2006, Rasberry was arrested, sentenced and convicted to six years in the Valley State Prison for Women on two counts of armed robbery. Rasberry left prison in 2012. She told Mic she was not thinking about the consequences of her decision when she broke the law at 18 but left prison inspired to bring awareness to what she calls the "ugly truth behind those walls." As a result, she has offered testimonies at the state capital about medical negligence inside of prisons, suicide, and alternatives to prison, such as ankle bracelets, rehabilitation programs, and preventative mental health services. She does outreach work three days a week in directly impacted communities, where she educates people about the realities of imprisonment—like the lack of basic provisions and physical and mental health treatment, especially for women.

Marlon Peterson spent 10 years, two months, and seven days in prison—his entire 20s. He was charged with second- degree murder but plead guilty to attempted robbery and assault in the first degree. During his incarceration, Peterson not only spent time thinking about the devastating impact of gun violence in his community but also wrote letters to young people in his hometown to engage with them on the issues. Since his release five years ago, Peterson has designed and implemented youth empowerment programs and worked to create safer communities, free of the violence that he witnessed growing up. He also earned an undergraduate degree from New York University. A published writer, he uses his platform as co-founder of The Precedential Group to humanize social justice issues.

Richard Spraggins' Interview
given by Timothy Strong
The Jordan Unit, January 3, 2020.

STRONG: So how are you living, Mr. Spraggins?
SPRAGGINS: Living the dream, my dude.

STRONG: WOW! That's a first; I never heard of anyone from our standing point say that "Prison" was a dream come true.
SPRAGGINS: Well, I tell convicts all the time that the circumstance don't make the man, the man makes the circumstance. It all depends on how you look at things. The way I see it, my body is the only thing that's
locked up, my mind is always free to create.

STRONG: So does that mean that you're actually glad that you came to prison?
SPRAGGINS: [Spraggins laughs] I can see it now. "We have a special—act now, and you can get five-to-10 years for a discounted price." But on the real, I don't think anyone in their right mind is willing to fill out an application to come to prison. But instead of crying over spilled milk, I think the best thing to do is take advantage of all the precious time that we have. Majority of the time, people in here only notice the things that we don't have but fail to recognize all the grand opportunities that we do have. Do you know how many times I've heard or read where someone on the outside said that they would do this and that only if they had enough time? From the very first, day I set foot in the pen, my vision was to come out stronger, smarter, and more enlightened. I made the decision, I made the commitment, and I focused on the vision day and day out. No, I'm not glad I came to prison—that would be a selfish statement considering the fact that I have children. But instead of folding, I allowed prison to be my 101 courses to reality.
That way, when I do get out of here, I can be a better father, a better husband, a better son, a better friend—basically a better human being. Right now is the practice field for my next return

because I don't want my past to define my future. I don't want to be remembered as a pimp or a "Can't Get Right" criminal. I want to be remembered as a great man who used my natural ability to influence others in a positive way.

STRONG: I can hear the conviction in your voice, Mr. Spraggins, so I can tell that you really mean what you say. However, does writing and your art help you stay focused?

SPRAGGINS: No doubt! Writing and art give me a way to keep the chaos of prison at bay and prevents it from devouring me. It's a resource that allows me to confront and understand my past, and it opens a way toward the future that's based not on fear or bitterness or apathy but on compassionate involvement. Not to mention, through both avenues I'm able to contribute
a verse.

STRONG: Sweet. I remember that line from the movie Hustle & Flow. But what do you enjoy doing the most, writing or your art?

SPRAGGINS: People always ask me, what's your favorite talent? But that's something like asking a parent of five children to name their favorite child. But I constantly find myself pulling out the old "I'm a writer" and "I'm an artist" card, but then there's always someone staring at me sideways as if I'm not worthy enough to carry such a sacred card in the wallet of my identity.

But I've always been the type of person that when someone tells me I can't do something, I'm eager as hell to go out and do it. Even if it's me telling myself, "you can't write a book," I want to prove to myself that I can.

STRONG: Do you enjoy writing? Is it hard for you? When I wrote my book, Dear Kim Kardashian, I know from my own personal experience that writer's block has a tendency to creep on you unexpectedly. Do you ever experience writer's block?

SPRAGGINS: When it comes to writing, no one realizes how hard it really is. It's fun, though! The weight on your brain and the constant awareness of writer's block are not all that enjoyable, though. But if something's that easy, it's not worth doing, right?

STRONG: True that! I guess that's why most people start books but rarely finish them because they didn't realize how much work it was. But how long have you been writing, and how did you get started?

SPRAGGINS: Over the course of the eight years I've been down, I read a countless number of books on a wide variety of topics, ranging from religion to physics, from business to How to Write Books. Prison alone has very few resources. I realized that the day I started this bid. I realized then the most valuable resources I could receive would be from literature, newspaper, magazines, and books. These would be the resources to help me accomplish my vision of writing because the first thing I had to do was get informed. Once I developed a broad perspective of the world and life in general, I began to write.
STRONG: Your first book 'Threat To The World' was pretty interesting. What inspired you to write it?

SPRAGGINS: I once thought of myself as a stomp-down pimp but didn't realize that those thoughts were actually derived from psychological issues. Whoever chooses to pimp, sell dope, con, steal, et cetera, over raising his children...has lost touch with reality. In other words, he has lost his damn mind! The book sounds like I'm glorifying the game until you make it to the end.

STRONG: Well, I get that. But I'm going to be honest with you. From reading this book "Pimp-N The Pen," I don't really understand your standing point towards white people. From one conception, it sounds like you are suggesting that we should embrace all races, but from the Willie Lynch speech and your poem "Slaves To The Devils," it almost sounds as if you are hinting that we should hate white people.

SPRAGGINS: Not at all, fam. I can't get on board of the hate train. Racism is a clear sign of ignorance because, in today's day and time if a person is a racist, more than likely, it's because they're uneducated. My sole purpose for writing some of the material that you are referring to is so I could open my people's eyes to the fact that what we're representing and dying for isn't even who we are. IT'S NOT OUR GAME. I'm not into all that hateful, inflammatory rhetoric. I'm more into illustrating a clear picture of who we are and who we are not. If a black man in the white man's penitentiary gains the full understanding of the fact that he is the true living God of this planet and the sole controller of the universe, then please believe fam, he will not return to a life of crime. Simply by gaining knowledge of self, he will begin to see crime as a petty, trifling act that, in fact, is beneath him. But the sad part of the game is that we will deny every notion of the fact that we are Gods of this earth, but we will swear up and down that we are gangstas, pimps, and thugs.

STRONG: Ok, that's where I have to disagree with you, bro. I know that I'm not a gangster, pimp, or a thug, but I'm not God either. I was raised as a Christian with Christian beliefs.

SPRAGGINS: Yeah, you and damn near the whole black race. And that includes Hispanics too. We were lied to fam. Our ancestors bought that lie. THERE IS NO MYSTERY GOD WAY UP IN THE SKY! Don't get it twisted, the Europeans are crafty people. They have been using silent weapons for control and conquer methods ever since they came to understand how powerful of a weapon it really is. Trust me, if they will go to the extent of using medicine, miseducation, and entertainment to control a mass population, then please understand that they will use religion too. We worship both aspects of what they consider good and evil. It's white supremacy at its finest. Black people follow all kinds of practices, habits, beliefs, and hang-ups that aren't ours. And whether they're good or bad, we don't worry about the consequences until it's too late. But my dude,

I'm going to hop off that subject because that's an entirely different book.

STRONG: Ok, cool. But what's the most important message you want your readers to learn or gain from reading this book "Pimp-N The Pen?"

SPRAGGINS: I want my readers to fully grasp the awareness that we are creators. Like I said in the beginning, there is a very low awareness level amongst convicts. In the state of Texas alone, mostly everyone is motivated by food.

They lie for it, they steal for it, they work for it, they hustle for it, and they wake up and go to sleep fiending for food. I want my readers to start Paying close attention with conscious awareness of their surroundings. That way they can peep the worthless, not-worth-mentioning motivations that surround them.

There's hardly any miracles being created here because everyone is on the same bullshit. I want the person reading this book to start thinking like a creator and stop thinking like a criminal. That includes stealing out of the kitchen! What, you have to survive? Well, roaches SURVIVE. Thrive and take your prison experience to the next level. Take your true potential to the highest level of victory. Never be average and never blend in with the deaf, dumb, and blind.

On the other hand, be great and achieve something that you can take home with you. Then, and only then, the question will not be: "Are you ready for the world?" The appropriate question will be: "Is the world ready for you?" For each and every last one of you who takes these words and your life seriously, I'll see you at the top. I'm out!

I don't know how many wonders of the world there are by now, but it is possible that (YOUR NAME) will someday join the list.

Richard Spraggins has always had a creative side—he began drawing at a very young age. His focus was on art for so many years. He expressed himself primarily through his artwork. Recently he found an overwhelming desire to write. He subsequently rediscovered things about himself that he had hidden deep within. We often hide who we are to make others comfortable. Then we get so comfortable being lost—it takes something or someone special to motivate us to find our true selves. The writing was just the catalyst for rediscovery that Richard needed. He is changing his world by using his time wisely by writing books and attending college. Richard wants to prove that mistakes do not determine your destiny. Come and experience Richard's writing and allow him to pull you into his world.

THREAT TO THE WORLD

THOMAS THREAT, WHO PREFERS TO BE CALLED BY HIS LAST NAME, IS THE OFFSPRING OF A WELL-RESPECTED MIDWESTERN PIMP. THREAT FINDS HIMSELF LOCKED-UP IN THE TEXAS DEPARTMENT OF CRIMINAL JUSTICE SYSTEM ON A 12-YEAR BID. THERE, HE RUNS INTO MACK WHO LACES HIM UP WITH THE ESSENTIAL REQUIREMENTS THAT ARE NEEDED TO SUCCEED—NOT ONLY IN THE INSIDE BUT ON THE OUTSIDE AS WELL.

THREAT'S BEAUTIFUL, DYNAMIC, AND VERY LOYAL SISTER MAYA HAS BEEN BY HIS SIDE FROM DAY ONE. MAYA IS THREAT'S BIGGEST FAN, BUT AS HE IS WILLING TO DO ANYTHING TO REKINDLE WHAT'S IN HIS BLOOD, THREAT HAS TO COME TO AN AWAKENING CONCLUSION OF WHAT'S THE MOST IMPORTANT FACTOR IN HIS LIFE.

IN THIS PSYCHOLOGICAL TWIST, A SAGA OF REALITY VERSUS FANTASY, THREAT WILL GENERALLY UNDERSTAND THAT THE VOICES INSIDE OF HIS HEAD COME WITH THE GAME.

BOTTOM LINE!! MONEY TALKS, BUT LOVE TALKS LOUDER.

AVAILABLE ON AMAZON AND BARNES & NOBLE
ON AMAZON ENTER ISBN: 1974399656
ON BARNES & NOBLE ENTER ISBN: 9781974899659

What I Want

I Am Powerful!
Whatever I set my mind on having,
I will have. Whatever I decide
to be, I will be.
The evidence is all around me.
The power of my WILL has brought me precisely
to where I am right now.
I have made choices. I have held my thoughts.
I have taken actions to create my current reality.
And I have the power to change it into whatever I
want it to be. With the choices I make, I am constantly
fulfilling the vision I have for my life.
If that does not seem to be the case—
Then I am deceiving myself about what I
really want. Because what I really truly
want, I will get!
What I truly wanted in the past; I already have.
If I want to build a billion-dollar business, I will
take the actions necessary to do it.

If I want to sit comfortably watching TV night after
night, I will take the actions necessary for that.

Don't be disappointed in my results—they're just the
outward manifestation of my priorities.

I will be sure of what I truly want

because I am sure to get it!

I have never been to jail, and I love what message you seem to be sending with the book. **An Incredibly inspiring book! I love how you used positive lessons from people like Malcolm X, Enemigo, and Wahida Clark it gives something to a community that it needs to know.**

Your story is seriously inspirational, not just saying that. So many people who are not locked up who are wasting their time with LeBron's stats and mindless gossip who could learn a thing or two from you.

Richard! Good luck, you have a marvelous message!

Great story, and very communicative throughout.

Cheers,

Tek

ABOUT THE AUTHOR

Richard Spraggins is the author of Threat To The World. A former pimp who was born in Chicago, Illinois, raised in Minneapolis, Minnesota, now writes from a Texas prison cell. Although gaining the reputation as a renowned artist, Richard now dedicates his life to showing the cause and effect (which is his and mostly everyone else's downfall) for staying true to the game.

You may contact the author through

Free To Create LLC

PO BOX 494375

Garland, Tx 75049-437

www.ingramcontent.com/pod-product-compliance
Lightning Source LLC
Chambersburg PA
CBHW081459040426

42446CB00016B/3306